PICTORIAL GUIDE
TO
PERENNIALS

by
M. Jane Coleman Helmer, Ph.D.
Karla S. Decker, B.S.

First Edition 1991

First Printing February, 1991

Second Printing April, 1991

Third Printing August, 1991

Fourth Printing January, 1992

ISBN 0-89484-051-7 Softcover
Library of Congress Catalog Card No. 90-91896

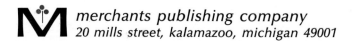

merchants publishing company
20 mills street, kalamazoo, michigan 49001

Printed in United States of America

CONTENTS

ACKNOWLEDGEMENTS

The authors wish to thank the following companies and individuals for their kind cooperation in providing information, encouragement, and advice throughout the preparation of this book:

Personnel at The Bailey Hortorium, Cornell University, Ithaca, NY: *Consultants.*
Mary Walters, Walters Gardens, Inc., Zeeland, MI: *Consultant.*
Dean Clark, Merchants Publishing Company: *Graphic Designer.*
Carri Law, Merchants Publishing Company: *Typographer.*

Photographs are from Merchants' comprehensive library of horticultural subjects and from the following sources: Argo Studios, Dean Clark, Peter Lindtner, Muriel Orans, Ben Pirrone, Dale VanEck, Walters Gardens, Inc., and Westland Photography.

INTRODUCTION TO PERENNIALS

Perennials are among the most useful plants for the home landscape. They are colorful and diverse, and can be used as more or less permanent features. While trees and shrubs — woody perennials — provide the outline and backdrop of the landscape, non-woody perennials can provide more detail and accents.

These plants, which are often called herbaceous or hardy perennials, come up year after year. Their life spans vary from just a few seasons to a decade or longer. Notable for their durability are Chinese peonies *(Paeonia lactiflora)*, a clump of which may flourish for 30 years. Among the short-lived perennials are *Delphinium* hybrids, which are spectacular for several seasons but which eventually lose vigor and need to be replaced: the beauty of their blooms and the plants' screening qualities make delphiniums well worth replacing every few years.

Many perennials described in this book are truly herbaceous, dying to the ground and growing fresh tops each spring from roots and stems that overwinter in the soil. Both Chinese peonies and delphiniums, as well as the majority of garden daisies (species of *Anthemis, Aster, Chrysanthemum, Coreopsis, Doronicum, Erigeron, Gaillardia, Heliopsis, Rudbeckia)* are examples of perennial herbs whose tops die completely in most zones. Other perennials, such as moss phlox *(Phlox subulata)* and periwinkle *(Vinca),* have woody stems that often survive winter freezes and from which fresh growth appears in spring. Still others, including coralbells *(Heuchera)* and *Bergenia*, display their attractive foliage throughout the winter months. In southern zones, herbaceous perennials such as columbine *(Aquilegia)* retain foliage through most or all of the winter.

Diverse colors, styles

Probably no other group of plants is represented by the vast range of height, spread, and flower and foliage forms that can be found among perennials. Some grow to a stately 8′ (2.4m) or more, while others creep over the ground, growing just 3-4″ (8-10cm) high. The clumps may spread, mound, or sprawl, or they may remain relatively narrow and concise year after year. Between these extremes is a myriad of varying shapes and sizes.

Flowers are produced in nearly all colors of the rainbow, with a variety of forms and shapes. Some grow as tall spikes; others are in daisy form. Star, bell, globe, tube, powderpuff, spider, and variations of these bloom shapes create interest in the garden from early spring until frost.

Foliage styles range from the simple grass-like leaves of garden pinks *(Dianthus)* to the more complex, lobed, and deeply cut leaves of Shasta daisy *(Chrysanthemum × superbum)*. Nearly every shade of green is represented, sometimes with variegations that stripe, edge, or mottle the leaves with gold or ivory for a two-tone effect. Such foliage gives plants ornamental value before and after flowering, and a number of perennials are grown strictly for their foliage quality.

Cultural needs vary

Today's perennials have their origins in nearly all parts of the world. The different soils and climates in which perennials can be grown are as varied as their origins. Although some are relatively specific as to their need for, say, well-drained soil or winter temperature tolerance, many perennials are very adaptable and will grow in a broad range of conditions. Such details are given in the descriptions of individual plants on pages 21-119.

Versatile Perennials

Because of their many differences in appearance and cultural requirements, perennials meet a wide range of growing needs and situations. Some varieties may lend themselves to a flower border, while others may look best in the rock garden. A number of perennials make good groundcovers, and still others flourish in the foreground of a bed or border. Perennial uses are shown in specific lists on pages 4-19; more details are given with individual plant copy (pages 21-119).

Perennials for all gardens

Perennials need relatively little maintenance. While annuals must be planted afresh each year, many perennials come up year after year with minimal or no added work. A single clump of yarrow *(Achillea)*, planted as an accent, will flourish for many years, undemanding, persistent, and reliable. Low maintenance groundcovers, such as bishop's weed *(Aegopodium)* and lamb's-ears *(Stachys)*, are especially good in a natural landscape planting; they maintain their vigor without being so invasive that they dominate and crowd out other plants. In more formal perennial plantings, maintenance requirements become greater: plants may need support or trimming, vigorous roots should be divided periodically, and tender favorites like *Dahlia* must be lifted and stored each winter.

Colorful Foliage

GRAY-GREEN or SILVERY
Achillea Yarrow
Artemisia Wormwood
Aurinia saxatilis Basket-of-gold
Centaurea montana Mountain Bluet
Chamaemelum nobile Roman Chamomile
Dianthus Pink, Carnation
Dicentra eximia Fringed Bleeding-heart
Eryngium Sea Holly
Lavandula angustifolia English Lavender
Macleaya cordata Plume Poppy
Salvia × superba Violet Sage
Santolina chamaecyparissus Lavender Cotton
Stachys byzantina Lamb's-ears
Yucca Adam's-needle, Soapwort

BLUE or BLUE-GRAY
Elymus arenarius Lyme Grass
Festuca (some) Fescue
Helictotrichon sempervirens Blue Oat Grass
Molinia caerulea Purple Moor Grass
Perovskia atriplicifolia Azure Sage
Ruta graveolens Rue

BRONZE, RED
Ajuga reptans (some) Carpet Bugle
Sedum (some) Stonecrop

VARIEGATED
Aegopodium podograria 'Variegatum' Snow-on-the-mountain
Ajuga reptans (some) Carpet Bugle
Cerastium tomentosum Snow-in-summer
Hosta (some) Plantain Lily
Lamium maculatum Spotted Deadnettle
Pachysandra terminalis 'Variegata'
      Variegated Japanese Spurge
Thymus × citriodorus (variegated forms) Variegated Thyme
Vinca (variegated forms) Periwinkle

Perennials as accents

Accent plantings are needed in every landscape that otherwise would be lacking significant features. The range of color, size, and style means there is at least one perennial for every situation — whether it be a balcony container or the focus of massed plantings or the end of a vegetable garden that's seen from the living room or the stony ground at one corner of the property.

Accent perennials are frequently used in combination plantings: a tall shrubby perennial with some other landscape feature such as a fence, or in a planting containing a small tree, shrub and/or conifer. Adam's-needle *(Yucca filamentosa)* and Black-eyed Susan *(Rudbeckia,* pictured below) are examples; these perennials also stand out well as solitary accents. Baby's-breath *(Gypsophila,* pictured at right), with its cloud-like show of blossoms, makes a useful contrast to conifers in foundation plantings. And in areas where it's winter hardy, a large clump of pampas grass *(Cortaderia selloana)* makes a stately specimen planting.

Gypsophila

Garden Fragrance

Foliage as well as flowers can provide a pleasing aroma. Perennials that have aromatic foliage are indicated with (F) in the following list.

Achillea (F) Yarrow
Anthemis (F) Golden Marguerite
Artemisia (F) Wormwood
Centranthus ruber Red Valerian
Cheiranthus cheiri English Wallflower
Chrysanthemum (F)
Cimicifuga Bugbane
Clematis paniculata
     Sweet Autumn Clematis

Convallaria majalis Lily-of-the-valley
Dianthus Pink, Carnation, Sweet William
Dictamnus albus Gas Plant
Filipendula Meadowsweet
Galium odoratum Sweet Woodruff
Hesperis matronalis Dame's-rocket
Iris germanica hybrids Bearded Iris
Lavandula angustifolia English Lavender
Lunaria annua Honesty
Lythrum Loosetrife
Melissa officinalis Lemon Balm
Mentha Mint
Monarda (F) Wild Bergamot
Nepeta Catmint

Oenothera Evening Primrose, Sundrops
Origanum vulgare (F) Marjoram
Paeonia Peony
Papaver (some) Poppy
Perovskia atriplicifolia (F) Azure Sage
Phlox (some)
Primula Primrose
Ruta graveolens (F) Rue
Salvia (F) Sage
Santolina chamaecyparissus (F)
     Lavender Cotton
Thymus (F) Thyme
Viola odorata Sweet Violet

Rudbeckia

Perennials in containers

Perennials adapt well in containers such as patio pots and windowboxes. The most suitable plants are low to medium height with upright or trailing habit, and that bloom over a long season so the containers remain attractive throughout the time they can be enjoyed. In containers, as in the garden, perennials can be combined with annuals.

Perennials for container plantings should be those that tolerate rapidly changing water content in well-drained soils. Moisture needs are greatest during hot dry periods when containers frequently need to be watered more than once each day. Because the volume of soil in containers is relatively small, plant roots are limited for both water and nutrient availability. To keep plants looking their best, a regular feeding program needs to be maintained. Excess salts are likely to build up in the soil during the season, so soil should be replaced when plants are repotted each year.

Perennials for containers

These plants are well-suited to growing in containers:

Achillea Yarrow
Aconitum Monkshood
Anemone ✕ hybrida Windflower
Anemone hupehensis var. japonica Japanese Anemone
Anthemis Golden Marguerite
Aquilegia Columbine
Aster (shorter varieties)
Campanula poscharskyana Serbian Bellflower
Canna Indian-shot
Centaurea montana Mountain Bluet
Cheiranthus cheiri English Wallflower
Chrysanthemum (shorter varieties)
Dianthus Pink, Carnation, Sweet William
Dicentra Bleeding-heart
Doronicum Leopard's-bane
Gaillardia ✕ grandiflora Blanketflower
Galeobdolon luteum Golden Deadnettle
Gypsophila Baby's-breath
Hedera Ivy
Hemerocallis Daylily
Heuchera Coralbells
Liatris Gayfeather
Lythrum Loosestrife
Monarda didyma Bee Balm
Oenothera Evening Primrose, Sundrops
Origanum vulgare Marjoram
Penstemon Beard-tongue
Phlox subulata Moss Pink
Primula Primrose
Rosmarinus officinalis Rosemary
Sempervivum Hen-and-chickens
Vinca Periwinkle
Viola Pansy, Violet

Lavandula species

Herb Gardens

A number of herbs are perennials that can form the basis for a complete herb garden that will supply culinary needs and fragrance all year. The best location for such a garden is in an area of good, well-drained soil, part of which is semi-shaded, and which is conveniently accessible from the kitchen.

Herbs

The following perennial herbs are described in this book:

Allium schoenoprasum Chives
Allium sativum Garlic
Artemisia absinthium Common Wormwood
Artemisia dracunculus Tarragon
Artemisia dracunculus var. sativa French Tarragon
Chamaemelum nobile Roman Chamomile
Galium odoratum Sweet Woodruff
Lavandula angustifolia English Lavender
Marrubium vulgare Horehound
Melissa officinalis Lemon Balm
Mentha Mint
Monarda Wild Bergamot
Nepeta Catmint
Origanum vulgare Marjorum
Rosmarinus officinalis Rosemary
Ruta graveolens Rue
Salvia officinalis Garden Sage
Satureja montana Winter Savory
Tanacetum vulgare Tansy, Golden-buttons
Thymus Thyme

Sempervivum

Mertensia virginica

Natural landscapes

Many perennials will naturalize among shrubs, wildflowers, and bulbs. In fact, a number of cultivated perennials such as cardinal flower *(Lobelia cardinalis)* and goatsbeard *(Aruncus)* are natives of North America. Natural landscapes, from prairie to woodland, can be planned for low maintenance and seasonal beauty as well as for food and cover for wildlife. Native and naturalized perennials or wildflowers, such as tickseed *(Coreopsis)*, that are relatively versatile are identified thus "**N**" in the plant listings on pages 21-119. Just as some cultivated perennials find their place in natural plantings, so can these perennial wildflowers be used in more formal settings.

Woodland Gardens

Woodland garden plants require sun and ample moisture early in the year, but can often tolerate shade and drier soil in summer. The SHADE — DRY CONDITIONS list includes perennials that are best able to survive with dry soil in both spring and summer; plants in this WOODLAND list need more moisture especially in spring. For additional perennials that may be suitable for woodland plantings, see the SHADE — CONSISTENT MOISTURE and SHADE — DRY CONDITIONS lists on page 15.

Aquilegia canadensis Wild Columbine
Arisaema triphyllum Jack-in-the-pulpit
Aruncus dioicus Goatsbeard
Chrysogonum virginianum Green-and-gold
Cimicifuga Bugbane
Dicentra Bleeding-heart
Epimedium Barrenwort
Erythronium Dog-tooth Violet
Gentiana Gentian
Geranium (some) Geranium, Cranesbill
Helleborus Christmas/Lenten Rose
Heuchera Coralbells
Iris (some)
Liriope Lilyturf
Mertensia virginica Virginia Bluebells
Myosotis sylvatica Woodland Forget-me-not
Phlox (some)
Polemonium Jacob's-ladder
Polygonatum Solomon's-seal
Primula Primrose (needs moist soil in hot regions)
Pulmonaria Lungwort
Sanguinaria canadensis Bloodroot
Tradescantia Spiderwort
Trillium Wake Robin
Viola Pansy, Violet

Trillium

Perennial borders and beds

Perennials have long been used in carefully thought-out flower gardens or in beds that provide beauty, fragrance, and flowers for cutting from spring until late autumn. Good planning helps minimize the maintenance needs of every garden planting. The traditional cottage garden that looks so natural is generally the result of well-planned groupings in which the individual plants neither crowd one another nor leave unsightly gaps once they have become established.

The traditional position for perennial borders and beds has been at the side or back of the home. Today's gardeners have expanded on this. While some landscapers may have reserved the front or public side of a house for a more formal appearance, others are including perennial plantings that add pleasing color and texture where all may enjoy them. An older home, for example, with the traditional narrow edgings and borders or foundation plantings of tired evergreens, can be revitalized when these planting spaces are reshaped, widened, or replaced entirely to accommodate colorful plantings that include perennials.

Another goal of today's landscaper and home gardener is to tie the garden to indoor living areas. For this, suitable garden sites are easily viewed from living areas within the home. The beds or borders are not necessarily fully visible from indoors: they serve as invitation to come outside where more of the landscape can be seen and enjoyed.

Many variations on the traditional perennial bed or border have appeared in recent years, each one to suit the environment and the needs of the homeowners. For example, pockets or groups of tender annuals are incorporated for seasonal variety. Each year, the perennials provide protection and background for the changing annual plantings. In addition, early spring color and attractive accents throughout the year can be achieved through the use of hardy bulbs such as snowdrops *(Galanthus)*, *Crocus*, and daffodils *(Narcissus)* among the perennials. Tender plants that should be lifted each fall *(Canna* and other lilies, for example) find shelter and may thrive longer among perennials.

Regardless of what shape a perennial garden takes, it is wise to provide an edging to prevent the encroachment of lawn grasses and possible mechanical damage to flowers from lawn equipment. Such an edging will also give the bed form. Bricks, tiles, slates, flagstones, railroad ties, landscape timbers, or plastic lawn edging can be used. Flagstones or decorative masonry blocks can also be used to provide a pathway into the garden for maintenance and cutting purposes.

Borders

Perennial borders have traditionally been long and narrow. Formal landscaping continues the tradition, with variations to suit individual sites and needs. Whatever the length or width of a border, it is usually backed by a building, fence, or evergreen screen to provide a suitable backdrop for the succession of color to come from early spring until autumn. Plants should be arranged in stairstep fashion so short plants are in front and taller ones are at the back. When planning a new or renewed perennial border, try to allow for an access path along the back — behind the tallest plants. A 36″ (90cm) minimum space from the back to the closest plants permits adequate air circulation and the best possible plant growth.

> Plants at the back of the border generally need more water than those at the front, not only because they are often taller but because of severe competition for soil moisture from shrub or tree hedges; a building, wall, or fence may shelter the back portion of the border from rain.

Beds

Free-standing perennial beds can be viewed from all sides. The beds can be any shape: round, oval, square, or the traditional rectangular oblong. For a pleasing all-around appearance, the tallest plants are usually placed in the center, with successively shorter ones towards the perimeter. If an island bed is used as a divider between work and play or leisure areas, the work side might include some plants that are used strictly for cutting, with the main attraction on the side that is seen from the indoor and/or outdoor living areas. The tallest plants in this example might be closer to the work area to allow more variety and depth to be seen from the main viewing area.

Planning perennial plantings

Winter months are usually the best time to begin planning any perennial planting. Armchair gardening, with the help of descriptive books and catalogs, gives time for reflection and visualization of an overall scheme, with or without detail. Graph paper can be used to plot the projected new plantings, with each variety drawn to scale: this is useful when determining quantities to order. Select varieties that meet the needs for color, blooming times, height, spread, and potential sources of fresh or dried bouquets.

Spacing perennials in group plantings

Massed perennials form a more pleasing effect when planted in groups rather than in rows. Spacing recommendations given on pages 21-119 are guides for both group and row (for a cutting garden) plantings. Even a single planting should be designed so that the plant's need for space, air, and soil type are met.

Color considerations

Bloom color affects the appearance of any planting. A bed or border that is dominated by bright colors (red, orange, yellow) will appear much closer to the viewer than one containing mostly cool tones (blue, gray, green). Whole borders can be designed with one basic tone — gray, for example. Or the combination of bright and cool colors achieves continuing interest, as the dominant color(s) changes through the growing season.

Flowers for cutting

Many perennials are useful for fresh-cut or dried flower design. Those that can be dried are noted in the following list.

Acanthus mollis Bear's-breech
Achillea Yarrow (dry)
Aconitum Monkshood
Alcea rosea Hollyhock
Alchemilla mollis Common Lady's-mantle
Anaphalis triplinervis
       Pearly Everlasting (dry)
Anemone Windflower
Anthemis Golden Marguerite
Aquilegia Columbine
Artemisia lactiflora White Mugwort
Asclepias tuberosa Butterfly Flower
Aster
Astilbe False Spirea
Baptisa australis False Indigo
Bergenia cordifolia Heartleaf Bergenia
Calamagrostis Reed Grass (dry)
Campanula persicifolia Peachleaf Bellflower
Campanula glomerata Clustered Bellflower
Catananche caerulea
       Blue Cupid's-dart (dry)
Centaurea Cornflower
Centranthus ruber Red Valerian

Chrysanthemum
Convallaria majalis Lily-of-the-valley
Coreopsis Tickseed
Cortaderia selloana Pampas Grass
Crocosmia ✕ crocosmiiflora Montbretia
Dahlia
Delphinium
Dianthus Pink, Carnation, Sweet William
Dicentra Bleeding-heart
Dictamnus albus Gas Plant (dry)
Digitalis Foxglove
Doronicum Leopard's-bane
Echinacea (dry)
Echinops Globe Thistle (dry)
Erigeron Fleabane
Eryngium Sea Holly
Eupatorium Boneset
Gaillardia ✕ grandiflora Blanketflower
Geum Avens
Gypsophila Baby's-breath (dry)
Hedera Ivy (foliage)
Helenium Sneezeweed
Helianthus Sunflower
Heliopsis helianthoides
       Sunflower Heliopsis
Helleborus Christmas/Lenten Rose
Heuchera Coralbells
Inula ensifolia Swordleaf Inula

Iris
Kniphofia uvaria Torch Lily
Lathyrus latifolius Everlasting Pea
Lavandula angustifolia
       English Lavender (dry)
Liatris Gay-feather (dry)
Lunaria annua Honesty (dry)
Lupinus Lupine
Lychnis Campion
Lysimachia (some) Loosestrife
Monarda Wild Bergamot
Paeonia lactiflora Chinese Peony
Physalis alkekengi Chinese-lantern (dry)
Physostegia virginiana Obedience
Polemonium caeruleum Jacob's-ladder
Polygonatum Solomon's-seal
Primula Primrose
Rudbeckia Coneflower
Scabiosa caucasica Pincushion Flower
Sidalcea Prairie Mallow
Solidago Goldenrod (dry)
✕ Solidaster luteus Hybrid Goldenrod
Stokesia laevis Stoke's Aster
Thalictrum Meadow Rue
Thermopsis False Lupine
Trollius Globeflower
Veronica (some) Speedwell
Viola Pansy, Violet

Preparation of soil

As with most gardening projects, soil preparation for perennials is best begun well ahead of planting time. An early start means that unwanted grassy and broad-leaved weeds can be eradicated. Large clumps can be removed by hand during digging, or they can be tilled under; perennial grasses should be removed and destroyed or composted. Fresh weed seedlings, often from seed brought to the surface during soil preparation, are easily killed by hoeing or cultivating in the days and weeks after soil has been prepared. Even small areas, where just a few or only one perennial will be planted, can be prepared ahead of time.

Early preparation — eight weeks ahead of planting would be ideal — is especially important if the soil structure and content need modification. Most perennials like a well-drained soil that is relatively high in organic content and available plant foods. The preferred pH is slightly acid to neutral (pH values of 5.5 to 7.0). Some adjustments to existing soil may be necessary, especially for a new garden planting.

The soil should be dug or tilled thoroughly to a depth of at least 12″ (30cm). The deeper it is cultivated, the better the soil will be for perennials. Roots will be able to penetrate more deeply and so will be able to withstand drought. A hard pan only 8-10″ (20-25cm) down may restrict development. While digging or tilling, add whatever is needed to improve both the soil structure and its pH and fertility.

To improve a heavy clay soil, work in peat moss, leaves, leaf mold, or other organic matter. If the soil contains a lot of close-knit clay and is fine-textured, gypsum (at 5 pounds per 100 square feet) will help create a more open and friable structure. If drainage is very poor or nonexistent, it may even be necessary to lay field drain tile at a depth of 24-36″ (60-90cm) for the removal of excess water; or the bed can be raised with added topsoil to ensure good drainage. For sandy soils, add compost, organic matter, or well-drained topsoil so that sufficient moisture will be retained in the root zone. These modifiers enable soil to provide the air and moisture needed by actively growing roots.

The quantity of modifier to apply, unless specified otherwise, should be one-third to one-half the volume of soil to be turned over. In other words, if the ground is to be dug or tilled to the optimum depth of 12″ (30cm), use a layer of organic matter 4-6″ (10-15cm) deep, spread over the surface before digging begins.

To adjust the soil pH or acidity, use recommended rates of limestone for a change from acid towards neutral, or sulfur or iron sulfate to bring an alkaline soil closer to the desired neutral or slightly acidic condition. This is the time, too, to add solid garden fertilizer with analysis of about 5-10-5 (low nitrogen, high phosphorus) at 3-5 pounds per 100 square feet. If undecayed leaves or straw are used as modifiers, also include some high nitrogen ammonium nitrate (2 pounds per 100 square feet) to avoid a sudden loss of nitrogen to the microorganisms that help these "raw" modifiers decay.

If chemical weedkillers are applied, the prepared ground must lie fallow for at least two weeks; check the product label for the correct recommendation.

Double Digging

Double digging can open up very tight soils to a depth of about 20″ (50cm). While it is a time-consuming and laborious operation, the long-term result of healthy perennial growth for many years can make double digging worth the effort. The subsoil is improved with modifers, and it can either be left under the original topsoil (Method A), or be lifted to the surface so the top 20″ (50cm) of soil is mixed together (Method B).

Double digging procedure

STEP 1 Starting at one end or side, remove the top 10″ (25cm) of soil from two 12″-wide (30cm) rows; place soil in wheelbarrow or on plastic so it is available to add to the other end or side of the plot (see diagram on opposite page for this and subsequent steps).

Method A	Method B
Subsoil stays below topsoil	*Lift subsoil to surface*
STEP 2 Subsoil unsuitable for mixing with topsoil (e.g. heavy clay or pure sand or limestone): modify subsoil structure but leave it underneath. Remove and reserve a third 12″ (30cm) row of topsoil.	**STEP 2** Subsoil suitable for mixing with topsoil. Dig out the lower 10″ (25cm) of soil — the subsoil — from the first 12″ (30cm) row, and set it aside for replacing the last row of subsoil at the end of the task.
STEP 3 Dig out the lower 10″ (25cm) of soil — the subsoil — from the first 12″ (30cm) row, and set it aside for replacing the last row of subsoil at the end of the task.	**STEP 3** Turn a third topsoil 12″ (30cm) row, with modifiers as needed, into the trench left by the first row of subsoil.
STEP 4 Spread subsoil modifiers over the surface of the second 12″ (30cm) row, and turn that row to mix and replace the first.	**STEP 4** Spread subsoil modifiers over the surface of the second row, and turn that row onto the top of the first row (topsoil beneath).
STEP 5 Turn the fourth 12″ (30cm) row of topsoil, with modifiers as needed, onto the top of the mixed subsoil in the first row.	

Repeat the last two steps with succesive 12″-wide (30cm), 10″-deep (25cm) rows: replace the final ones with topsoil and subsoil reserved from the first few rows.

Double Digging
STEP 1 (Methods A and B)

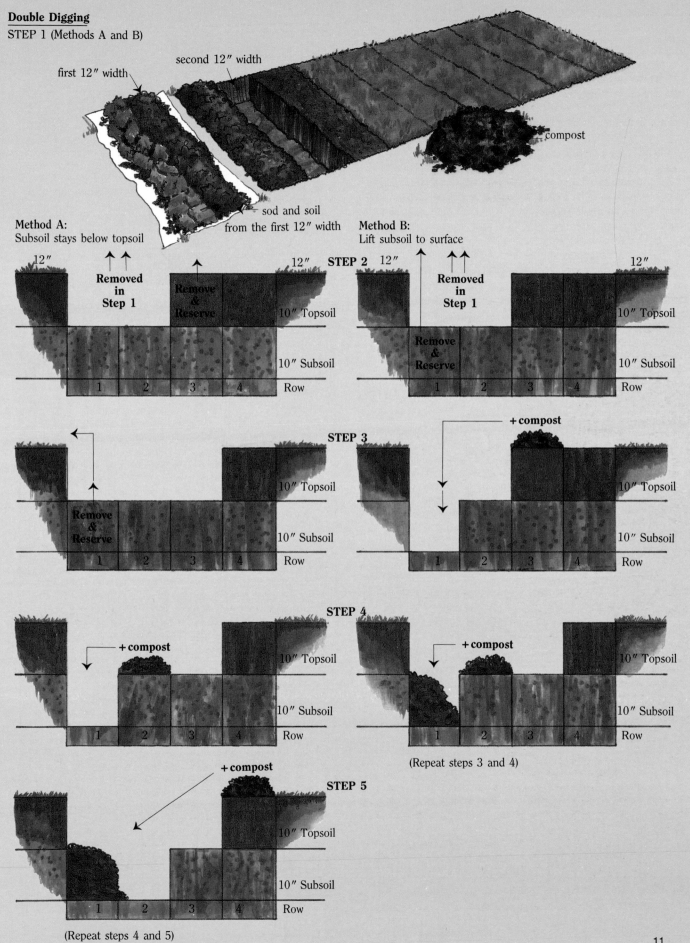

first 12″ width

second 12″ width

compost

sod and soil
from the first 12″ width

Method A:
Subsoil stays below topsoil

Method B:
Lift subsoil to surface

STEP 2

12″

Removed
in
Step 1

Remove
&
Reserve

12″

10″ Topsoil

10″ Subsoil

1 2 3 4 Row

12″

Removed
in
Step 1

12″

Remove
&
Reserve

10″ Topsoil

10″ Subsoil

1 2 3 4 Row

STEP 3

Remove
&
Reserve

10″ Topsoil

10″ Subsoil

1 2 3 4 Row

+ compost

10″ Topsoil

10″ Subsoil

1 2 3 4 Row

STEP 4

+ compost

10″ Topsoil

10″ Subsoil

1 2 3 4 Row

+ compost

10″ Topsoil

10″ Subsoil

1 2 3 4 Row

(Repeat steps 3 and 4)

+ compost

STEP 5

10″ Topsoil

10″ Subsoil

1 2 3 4 Row

(Repeat steps 4 and 5)

11

Planting Perennials

New plants are usually made available from the start of the recommended planting period. Those shipped from a distant nursery should also arrive during the correct season — from early spring in the North, or during both fall and spring in southern zones. Immediate planting is best, though may not always be possible. If newly purchased and delivered perennials cannot be planted right away, store them in a cool (but not freezing) dark place after opening the tops of plastic bags for aeration. Plant as soon as conditions are good.

Bare root perennials: Open packages and soak roots in water or a VERY dilute fertilizer solution (no more than 25% recommended strength) for 12-24 hours. Remove from liquid and replace in the waxed or plastic shipping compartments, or lay plants in box of damp peat moss. Repeat in 2-3 days if perennials still cannot be planted. This practice pays off in getting the plants established sooner and more rapidly than those whose roots (and stems) remain dry before planting.

Perennials in containers with soil: Add moisture as needed.

Set out the individual plants in their containers or in batches that are packed together (still in their plastic bags to prevent drying out, or, for bare root perennials, in water), on or near their planting positions. Then, handling the plants one at a time so roots have the least exposure to the drying air, plant. Dig holes big enough for the root systems and with one hand hold each plant in its hole so that the junction of roots and stem(s) or crown will be at or slightly below the soil surface. With the other hand, tumble loose soil around roots and other underground parts. Gently firm the soil over or around smaller perennials; larger plants should be tamped or firmed in more securely. Water each newly planted perennial so soil and roots settle in together; in dry conditions, plants are best puddled in with plenty of water, so that surrounding soil is moistened.

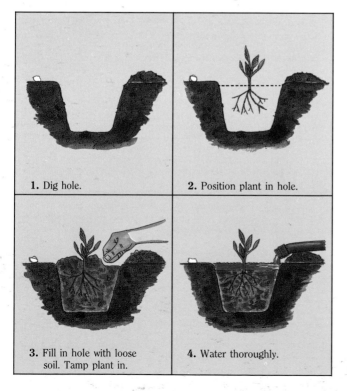

1. Dig hole.

2. Position plant in hole.

3. Fill in hole with loose soil. Tamp plant in.

4. Water thoroughly.

Moisture Tolerant Perennials

These plants tolerate extra-moist or boggy soils; most of them also thrive in moderately moist conditions, so they can be planted in a variety of soils.

Aconitum Monkshood
Aegopodium Bishop's Weed
Aquilegia Columbine
Arenaria montana Mountain Sandwort
Aruncus Goatsbeard
Asarum Wild Ginger
Astilbe False Spirea
Baptisia australia Blue False Indigo
Bergenia cordifolia Heartleaf Bergenia
Boltonia asteroides White Boltonia
Brunnera macrophylla Heartleaf Brunnera
Calamagrostis Reed Grass
Caltha palustris Marsh Marigold
Campanula Bellflower
Chelone lyonii Turtlehead
Cimifuga Bugbane
Coreopsis rosea Rose Coreposis
Deschampsia caespitosa Tufted Hair Grass
Digitalis Foxglove
Epimedium Barrenwort
Eupatorium (some) Boneset
Euphorbia griffithii Griffith's Spurge
Filipendula Meadowsweet
Gentiana Gentian
Geranium sanguineum Blood-red Cranesbill
Glyceria maxima 'Variegata' Manna Grass
Helenium Sneezeweed
Hemerocallis Daylily
Hosta Plantain Lily
Houttuynia cordata Chameleon Plant
Iberis Candytuft
Inula ensifolia Swordleaf Inula
Iris (some)
Liatris Gay-feather
Liriope Lilyturf
Lobelia cardinalis Blue Cardinal Flower
Lysimachia Loosestrife
Lythrum Loosestrife
Mentha Mint
Mertensia virginica Virginia Bluebells
Monarda Wild Bergamot
Myosotis scorpioides Water Forget-me-not
Nepeta Catmint
Osmunda claytoniana Interrupted Fern
Paeonia suffruticosa Tree Peony
Phalaris arundinacea var. picta Ribbon Grass
Phlox (some)
Physostegia virginiana Obedience
Polemonium Jacob's-ladder
Polygonatum Solomon's-seal
Polygonum Knotweed
Primula japonica Japanese Primrose
Pulmonaria Lungwort
Ranunculus repens Buttercup
Rodgersia aesculifolia Fingerleaf Rodgersia
Sanguinaria canadensis Bloodroot
Sanguisorba Burnet
Symphytum Comfrey
Thalictrum Meadow Rue
Tiarella False Miterwort
Tradescantia Spiderwort
Trillium Wake-robin
Trollius Globeflower

Continuing Care of Perennials

Watering and Fertilizing

The need to water perennials varies from place to place as well as from month to month. Where watering is needed much of the time, a more or less permanent system of soaker hoses laying on the ground would be best.

Fertilization for perennials is usually needed once or twice during the growing season. Make one early summer application of a granular 5-10-5 formulation at a lighter application rate than during soil preparation (2 pounds per 100 square feet), or one or two liquid fertilizer applications (use at half the recommended rate to avoid burning tender young shoots and overdosing with nitrogen which leads to excessive leafy growth).

For established perennial plantings, surface or liquid applications of an all-around garden fertilizer two or three times during the year will provide adequate amounts of plant food. One application should be in early spring while plants are still dormant, another six weeks into the growing season, and the third in mid- to late summer.

Foliar sprays of dilute liquid fertilizer will bring almost immediate though short-term results; for the best results when plants show signs of nutrient deficiencies, combine foliar feeding with soil applications. A regular fertilization program, though, should ensure healthy plant growth and development.

Weed Control

While perennials are small, it's an easy task to hand-weed or hoe lightly between the plants to prevent weeds from becoming established and from competing with the perennials for moisture and nutrients. As perennials grow and spread, weeds will be fewer. Remove those that do grow so the perennials can continue their unrestricted development.

A mulch of shredded bark, applied to the bare and weed-free soil between (but not touching) perennials, will help not only with weed control but with moisture conservation.

Mulches

Mulching with rotted bark, peat moss, or other organic material will improve the air/water relationship in the soil. Most perennials also perform better the following spring if an application of straw, leaves, or evergreen boughs has been made in late autumn to protect against winter damage (with a supply of nitrogen as needed to assist when unrotted straw and leaves start to decay — see Preparation of Soil for Perennials on page 10). The need for protection is greatest where the planting site is at the northern limit of a variety's hardiness rating. Such ratings have been included for each perennial listed on pages 21-119, and the USDA Hardiness Zone Map on page 128 can help gardeners determine which perennials will survive in their locales.

Staking/Support

Taller-growing perennials such as some varieties of *Aster* need support to prevent their flopping over. While the plants are still fairly short and before they start to fall, insert branching twigs among the foliage and between plants. Subsequent growth will cover the twigs. For the individual heavy stems of, say, *Delphinium* or hollyhock *(Alcea rosea)*, use single canes, stakes, or other supports. More than one tie per stem will be needed as the plant grows.

Dry Soils and Hot Dry Conditions

Many of the following perennials grow well in dry soils. Most can tolerate extreme heat in dry conditions (see next paragraph), but those that require watering during hot periods (W) or that will tolerate dry soils only in cooler climates (C) are noted here.

Heat tolerant plants can withstand long periods (up to 2 months) of full sun in temperatures exceeding 90°F (32°C). These plants survive best in soil that is free of competing roots and that has a surface mulch to protect the perennials' roots from the scorching sun as well as to retain any moisture.

Acaena microphylla New Zealand Bur
Achillea Yarrow
Amsonia tabernaemontana (C)
   Willow Amsonia
Anaphalis triplinervis Pearly Everlasting
Anchusa Alkanet, Bugloss
Antennaria Pussy-toes
Anthemis (W) (C) Golden Marguerite
Arabis (W) (C) Rock Cress
Armeria maritima Thrift, Sea Pink
Arrhenatherum elatius var. bulbosum
   (C) Tuber Oat Grass

Artemisia Wormwood
Aurinia saxatilis (C) Basket-of-gold
Baptisia tinctoria Yellow False Indigo
Campanula poscharskyana (W)
   Serbian Bellflower
Catananche Cupid's-dart
Cerastium tomentosum Snow-in-Summer
Ceratostigma plumbaginoides Leadwort
Chamaemelum nobile Roman Chamomile
Chrysanthemum parthenium
   (W) Feverfew
Chrysanthemum × superbum
   Shasta Daisy
Coreopsis verticillata
   Threadleaf Coreopsis
Coronilla varia Crown Vetch
Cortaderia selloana Pampas Grass
Dianthus (W) Pink, Carnation
Echinacea purpurea Purple Coneflower
Echinops Globe Thistle
Elymus arenarius Lyme Grass
Erigeron Fleabane
Eryngium Sea Holly
Euphorbia (some) Spurge
Festuca (W) (C) Fescue
Gaillardia × grandiflora Blanketflower
Geranium (some) Cranesbill
Gypsophila paniculata Baby's-breath
Helianthemum Sun Rose
Helictotrichon sempervirens
   Blue Oat Grass
Hemerocallis Daylily

Iris (some)
Kniphofia uvaria Torch Lily
Lavandula angustifolia English Lavender
Leontopodium alpinum (C) Edelweiss
Liatris Gay-feather
Linum Flax
Lupinus perennis Wild Lupine
Lychnis viscaria German Catchfly
Malva Mallow
Miscanthus (W) (C) Silver Grass
Nepeta Catmint
Oenothera (some)
   Evening Primrose, Sundrops
Penstemon Beard-tongue
Petrorhagia saxifraga Tunic Flower
Phlox subulata Moss Pink
Platycodon grandiflorus Balloon Flower
Potentilla (W) Cinquefoil
Rudbeckia (W) Coneflower
Salvia Sage
Santolina Lavender Cotton
Saponaria ocymoides Rock Soapwort
Sedum Stonecrop (not all tolerate heat)
Sempervivum Hen-and-chickens
Solidago Goldenrod
Stachys byzantina Lamb's-ears
Thermopsis False Lupine
Tradescantia Spiderwort
Verbena
Yucca Adam's-needle, Soapwort

Trimming

Dead-heading (removal of dead flowers) and trimming off damaged parts during the growing season will maintain neat, trim, long-blooming perennials.

Fall Cleanup, Winter

When top growth has died back, trim for neatness as desired, and clean out weeds before they become established. Fall is the best time to lift and divide spring and summer flowering perennials in all but the coldest climates. Otherwise, divide perennials in spring. Dead top growth may either be removed (necessary if it is likely to harbor fungus and insects) or left as a protective mulch for the underground parts during winter. If it is trimmed back to within a few inches of the ground, apply a winter mulch after the ground has frozen; this will protect against alternate thawing and freezing which tend to lift plants out of the soil. Remove any remaining tops and the winter mulch in very early spring.

Hosta Frances Williams'

Shade — consistent moisture

All plants listed here will grow well in partially shaded locations; those that will tolerate or prefer deep shade are noted (S).

Acanthus Bear's-breech
Aconitum Monkshood
Adenophora Ladybells
Aegopodium (S) Bishop's Weed
Ajuga Bugleweed
Alchemilla Lady's-mantle
Anemone Wildflower
Aquilegia Columbine
Arenaria Sandwort
Arisaema triphyllum Jack-in-the-pulpit
Arrhenatherum elatius var. bulbosum Tuber Oat Grass
Artermisia lactiflora White Mugwort
Aruncus Goatsbeard
Asarum (S) Wild Ginger
Astilbe False Spirea
Athyrium filix-femina (S) Lady Fern
Brunnera macrophylla (S) Heartleaf Brunnera
Campanula Bellflower
Chelone lyonii Turtlehead
Chrysogonum (S) Goldenstar
Cimicifuga (S) Bugbane
Convallaria majalis (S) Lily-of-the-valley
Dicentra Bleeding-heart
Digitalis Foxglove
Epimedium (S) Barrenwort
Erythronium Dog-tooth Violet
Filipendula Meadowsweet
Galeobdolon luteum (S) Golden Deadnettle
Gaura lindheimeri White Gaura
Gentiana Gentian
Hakonechloa macra
Hedera (S) Ivy
Helleborus Christmas/Lenten Rose
Heuchera Coralbells
Hosta (S) Plantain Lily
Imperata cylindrica 'Rubra' Japanese Blood Grass
Liriope (S) Lilyturf
Lysimachia punctata Yellow Loosestrife
Mertensia virginica (S) Virginia Bluebells
Monarda Wild Bergamot
Myosotis Forget-me-not
Osmunda claytoniana (S) Interrupted Fern
Pachysandra terminalis (S) Japanese Spurge
Papaver nudicaule Iceland Poppy
Phlox divaricata Wild Blue Phlox
Polemonium Jacob's-ladder
Polygonatum (S) Solomon's-seal
Primula Primrose
Pulmonaria Lungwort
Pulsatilla vulgaris European Pasqueflower
Ranunculus repens (S) Creeping Buttercup
Sanguinaria canadensis Bloodroot
Symphytum caucasicum Blue Comfrey
Thalictrum Meadow Rue
Tiarella (S) False Miterwort
Trillium (S) Wake-robin
Trollius Globeflower
Vinca (S) Periwinkle
Viola Pansy, Violet
Waldsteinia (S) Barren Strawberry

Shade — dry conditions

Dry shaded areas are among the most challenging of places in which to garden. Not only is sunlight lacking, but soil moisture is exhausted by neighboring trees and shrubs or by nearby structures. The soil itself may be poor and dusty. Added organic matter will improve the soil and its moisture-retaining capacity, and regular watering and feeding will help supply the plants' needs. Even so, with vigorous competition from trees and shrubs, soil often remains dry.

Plants in this list are best able to tolerate dry shade. Those that tolerate or prefer deep shade are noted (S).

Adonis amurensis Amur Adonis
Anaphalis triplinervis Pearly Everlasting
Convallaria majalis Lily-of-the-valley
Epimedium (S) Barrenwort
Geranium (some) Cranesbill
Hosta (S) Plantain Lily
Lamium maculatum (S) Spotted Deadnettle
Pachysandra terminalis (S) Japanese Spurge
Pulmonaria saccharata Bethlehem Sage
Stachys byzantina Lamb's-ears
Symphytum grandiflorum Large-flowered Comfrey
Vinca Periwinkle

Aegopodium podograria 'Variegatum'

Perennials as Groundcover Plants

Groundcover plants come from four major plant groups: shrubs, conifers, woody vines, and perennials. They all provide the similar benefits of landscape feature as well as anchor, erosion control, protection of more tender plants, and modification of the environment. Perennial groundcovers are versatile and are especially useful where quick cover is needed.

Replace grass in landscape

Grass is the most familiar groundcover for tying together the landscape elements (trees and shrubs, buildings, fences, paved areas). Conservation-wise and low maintenance gardening makes use of other living groundcovers except in high traffic and play areas. And in some places grass may be impractical from either a maintenance or a visual standpoint; other perennial groundcover plants can be used to great advantage. For instance, on a steep embankment which is nearly impossible to mow, a cover of moss phlox *(Phlox subulata,* pictured on opposite page) or periwinkle *(Vinca)* provides a welcome alternative to grass. In a heavily shaded area, spreading bugleweed *(Ajuga,* pictured at right) can replace weak grass. The sun-loving evergreen candytuft *(Iberis sempervirens)* or silveredge bishop's weed *(Aegopodium podograria* 'Variegatum', pictured above) thrive in conditions that could burn out regular grass. And creeping Jennie *(Lysimachia nummularia)* does better than grass in damp areas.

Use in other areas

Some parts of the landscape naturally suit non-grass groundcovers. One example is the slim strip of soil between house and path or driveway. Another narrow area is near the foundation between shrubs or conifers. A perennial ground-cover planted beneath a fence softens the stark lines of the fence, and the homeowner does not have the repetitive chore of handtrimming grass around the fenceposts.

Ajuga genevensis

Control Erosion

Groundcovers prevent soil erosion in two ways. First, those with dense branching growth such as lavender cotton *(Santolina,* pictured at right) reduce the force of raindrops by breaking up each drop into smaller droplets that, rather than bounce or run off the soil surface, soak in gradually. Second, a number of perennial groundcovers root from rapidly spreading stems or stolons, binding the soil so it is less likely to blow or be washed away; examples here are English Ivy *(Hedera helix),* spring cinquefoil *(Potentilla tabernaemontani),* and mother-of-thyme *(Thymus serpyllum).* These are ideal for embankment plantings. If a slope is too great for the soil to hold before the new planting has become established, temporary or permanent artificial slope stabilizers such as rock or wood terraces across the slope may be needed.

Santolina chamaecyparissus

Phlox subulata in bloom with *Sedum*

Prevent mechanical damage

Perennial groundcovers can also act as protective barriers for trees and shrubs that are likely to be damaged by lawnmowers. An edging of lavender cotton *(Santolina,* pictured above), for example, eliminates the need to mow, sweep, or spread close to these permanent landscape plantings.

Modify environment

Groundcover plants serve to modify the environment for neighboring plants: low-growing perennials such as Lily-of-the-valley *(Convallaria)* and periwinkle *(Vinca),* teamed with *Clematis* vines or *Rhododendron,* provide the shade and moisture necessary to keep roots cool — essential for the growth of these shallow-rooted plants. In the same way, groundcovers cool the home environment. When sunbaked areas around the house are planted with drought tolerant groundcovers such as stonecrop *(Sedum),* the soil surface temperatures are reduced. Transpiration from plant foliage also cools the atmosphere.

Groundcover perennials

Achillea tomentosa Woolly Yarrow
Aegopodium Bishop's weed
Ajuga Bugleweed
Alchemilla alpina
    Mountain Lady's-mantle
Antennaria Pussy-toes
Arabis Rock Cress
Arenaria Sandwort
Armeria maritima Thrift, Sea Pink
Artemisia schmidtiana
    Silver Mound Artemisia
Asarum Wild Ginger
Aubrieta deltoidea Purple Rock Cress
Bergenia cordifolia Heartleaf Bergenia
Cerastium tomentosum Snow-in-summer
Ceratostigma plumbaginoides Leadwort
Chamaemelum nobile Roman Chamomile
Clematis paniculata
    Sweet Autumn Clematis
Convallaria majalis Lily-of-the-valley
Coronilla varia Crown Vetch
Dianthus (some) Pink

Dicentra (some) Bleeding-heart
Duchesnea indica Mock Strawberry
Epimedium Barrenwort
Euonymus fortunei 'Colorata'
    Purpleleaf Wintercreeper
Galeobdolon luteum Golden Deadnettle
Galium odoratum Sweet Woodruff
Geranium (some) Cranesbill
Gypsophila repens
    Creeping Baby's-breath
Hedera Ivy
Hosta Plantain Lily
Houttuynia cordata Chameleon Plant
Hypericum calycinum St.-John's-wort
Iberis Candytuft
Lamium maculatum Spotted Deadnettle
Lathyrus latifolius Everlasting Pea
Liriope Lilyturf
Lysimachia nummularia Creeping Jennie
Mentha pulegium Pennyroyal
Nepeta Catmint
Oenothera missouriensis Ozark Sundrops

Pachysandra terminalis Japanese Spurge
Papaver nudicaule Iceland Poppy
Petrorhagia saxifraga Tunic Flower
Phlox (some)
Polemonium reptans
    Creeping Jacob's-ladder
Polygonum Knotweed
Potentilla tabernaemontani
    Spring Cinquefoil
Ranunculus repens Creeping Buttercup
Santolina Lavender Cotton
Saponaria ocymoides Rock Soapwort
Sedum (some) Stonecrop
Stachys byzantina Lamb's-ears
Symphytum grandiflorum
    Large-flowered Comfrey
Thymus Thyme
Tiarella False Miterwort
Verbena (some)
Veronica (some) Speedwell
Vinca Periwinkle
Viola odorata Sweet Viola

17

Perennials for Rock Gardens

The rock garden has long been a favorite way to display low-growing perennials and herbs. Not only can it make use of an otherwise little used hillside location, but, when skillfully constructed, such a garden can give the appearance of a natural outcropping of rock. Where there is no hillside, a relatively flat area can be built up with soil and rocks to provide the well-drained, stony conditions needed by many rock garden plants. Tilt the flatter rocks or slabs into the slope to catch moisture and to channel it towards plant roots.

Perennials most attractive in rock gardens are those that grow to a height of 12-15″ (30-38cm). Some are upright growers, others are clump formers, and many creep or trail. The specialty group of Alpines originated above 3,200 feet in mountainous areas of the world; these and other suitable perennials share a need for well-drained soils and full sun. To meet this need, rock gardens should not be shaded and plants should be far enough away from shrubs or trees to avoid competition for available light and moisture. Position plants in a hilly rock garden according to their light and moisture needs, keeping those that grow best in dry conditions near the top of the slope.

Retaining walls

Rock walls may be built to support steeply sloping banks or as part of a garden terracing project. Built to lean into the slope, these mortarless walls will last for many years. Perennial plants, set into pockets between the stones, add beauty and help stabilize embankment soil. Most creeping and trailing plants that are listed for rock gardens can be used.

Perennials for rock gardens

The following list includes perennials for all sizes and scales of rock gardens; many of them can also be grown at the front of a border or raised bed. Cultural needs and illustrations are shown on pages 21 - 119.

Acaena microphylla New Zealand Bur
Achillea tomentosa Woolly Yarrow
Adonis
Aethionema Stonecress
Ajuga genevensis Geneva Bugleweed
Antennaria Pussy-toes
Anthemis marschalliana
   Marshall Camomile
Aquilegia flabellata Fan Columbine
Arabis Rock Cress
Arenaria Sandwort
Armeria maritima Thrift, Sea Pink
Aruncus aethusifolius
   Miniature Goatsbeard
Aster alpinus Alpine Aster
Aubrieta deltoidea Purple Rock Cress

Aurinia saxatilis Basket-of-gold
Bellis perennis English Daisy
Bergenia cordifolia Heartleaf Bergenia
Campanula (some) Bellflower
Cerastium tomentosum Snow-in-summer
Ceratostigma plumbaginoides Leadwort
Cheiranthus cheiri English Wallflower
Chrysogonum virginianum
   Green-and-gold
Coreopsis auriculata 'Nana'
   Dwarf Mouse Ear Coreopsis
Corydalis lutea Yellow Corydalis
Dianthus Pink, Carnation, Sweet William
Dicentra Bleeding-heart
Erigeron Fleabane
Euonymus fortunei 'Kewensis'
   Wintercreeper
Euphorbia myrsinites Myrtle Euphorbia
Festuca Fescue
Gentiana Gentian
Geranium (dwarf forms) Cranesbill
Geum × **borisii** Boris Avens
Gypsophila repens Creeping Baby's-breath
Helianthemum Sun Rose

Herniaria glabra Herniary
Hypericum calycinum St.-John's-wort
Iberis Candytuft
Imperata cylindrica 'Rubra'
   Japanese Blood Grass
Incarvillea delavayi Hardy Gloxinia
Inula ensifolia Swordleaf Inula
Iris (some)
Leontopodium alpinum Edelweiss
Linum Flax
Myosotis alpestris Alpine Forget-me-not
Nierembergia repens White Cupflower
Phlox stolonifera Creeping Phlox
Phlox subulata Moss Phlox
Platycodon grandiflorus var. mariesii
   Dwarf Balloon Flower
Potentilla Cinquefoil
Primula Primrose
Pulsatilla vulgaris European Pasqueflower
Saponaria ocymoides Rock Soapwort
Sedum Stonecrop
Sempervivum Hen-and-chickens
Thymus Thyme
Tricyrtis Toad Lily

The Ornamental Grasses

Ornamental grasses are useful in home and commercial landscapes because of their relatively low maintenance and interesting foliage that contrasts well with that of shrubs and flowering perennials. Their heights range from less than 12″ (30cm) to varieties growing 10′ (3m) or more. A number of these grasses are extremely hardy, providing year round displays. The majority should be planted in well-drained soils, and mulched during winter in the north to help assure vigorous growth the following spring. Taller varieties should be cut in the early spring to encourage new growth and for a fresh appearance.

Todays's uses for ornamental grasses are little different than those employed by Far Eastern gardeners in earlier times. Low-growing clump or mound styles are useful as bed edging, accents in a rock garden, or as groundcover. Blue fescue *(Festuca ovina* var. *glauca)*, with compact habit and stiff grassy blades radiating from the base, form dense mounds. Tuber oat grass *(Arrhenatherum elatius* var. *bulbosum)* is similar though with a softer, cascading, variegated foliage, and a tolerance of shade. A taller clump is formed by rose fountain grass *(Pennisetum alopecuroides)*, whose ornamental fluffy plumes of silvery-rose flowers are borne from mid- to late summer. This is a good accent grass in the perennial garden, and the flowers can be cut for drying and arranging.

Medium height range ornamental grasses are used near the back of a border, with shrubs, and may be prized for dried arrangements. For example, maiden grass *(Miscanthus sinensis* 'Gracillimus') produces rich green foliage and tall spikes of feathery, fine-textured creamy-white flowers; if left in the garden over winter, foliage and plumes turn an attractive golden color. Another in this group is variegated fountain grass *(M. sinensis* 'Zebrinus'), spectacular with its gold and green striped leaves and feathery pink and beige plumes. This one tolerates some shade and does well in damp locations, making it valuable near ponds or in low areas of the garden.

The taller ornamental grasses are often used singly as specimens in the landscape, or with several clumps making an effective screen. They provide good backgrounds for shorter flowering plants. One of the tallest is pampas grass *(Cortaderia selloana)*, which grows to a height of 8-12′ (2.4-3.6m). This narrow-leaved grass produces large plumes of creamy-white or rose flowers in September and October. While reliably hardy only in zones 6 or 7 through 10, it will survive in portions of more northerly zones. The hardier plume grass *(Erianthus ravennae)* is reliable to zone 5 and grows at least as tall as pampas grass. Their plumes are attractive in dried arrangements.

A number of perennial ornamental grasses are included among the plants described on pages 21-119 of this book.

GUIDE TO PERENNIALS: PLANT DESCRIPTIONS

The perennials described on the following pages are arranged alphabetically by botanical name. The common name or names are given with each entry. For quick reference, all of these names (both common and botanical) can be found in the index to plant names on pages 120 through 127.

Every genus or group of plants is illustrated with at least one full color photograph. Cultivar listings have been restricted to those that are usually readily available, so the book can include as many perennial subjects as possible.

Each plant description includes one or more symbols for recognition of the perennial's light requirements and other specific details.

○ = Full Sun	♠ = Evergreen
◐ = Partial Shade	N = Native or Naturalized Plant
● = Shade	⚐ = Ornamental Grass
⋎ = Groundcover	✕ = Cut Flowers

Acaena microphylla

Acanthus mollis

Achillea filipendula

ACAENA (a-SEE-na) ○ ♠

A. microphylla (my-kroh-FIL-a)
New Zealand Bur

Low-growing evergreen with bronze-green foliage; mounds 6-8″ (15-20cm). Moist or dry soil. Good in rock gardens. Inconspicuous late summer flowers are followed by colorful red-spiny fruits (burs). Give winter protection in northern zones.

Zones: 6-10
Spacing: 12-15″ (30-38cm)
Propagation: division in spring, seed in fall

ACANTHUS (a-KAN-thus) ○ ◑ ✂

A. mollis (MOL-is)
Bear's-breech

Elegant border plant with long, deeply cut foliage that mounds to 3-4′ (0.9-1.2m) high. Best in well-drained soil. Semi-evergreen in southern zones. White and lilac colored flowers on 18″ (45cm) erect spikes appear in late spring and early summer.

Zones: 8-10
Spacing: 18-24″ (45-60cm)
Propagation: seed, root cuttings, division

ACHILLEA (a-KIL-ee-a) ○ ✂
Yarrow

Easy to grow, drought-tolerant plants. Best in well-drained soil. Shorter varieties good for rock gardens and foreground, taller ones rarely need support in middle and background plantings. Fern-like foliage has pungent odor. Flowers usually small but numerous, in flat-topped or rounded cluster; excellent for dried arrangements.

Zones: 3-10
Spacing: 12-24″ (30-60cm): see individual species
Propagation: division in spring or fall, seed (species), root cuttings

A. ✕'Coronation Gold'
Coronation Gold Yarrow

Mounds to 36″ (90cm). Gray-green foliage. Flowers for long period from late spring to summer; flat, mustard-yellow clusters 3-4″ (8-10cm) across; cut flowers dry well. Space 24″ (60cm) apart.

A. filipendula (fi-li-PEN-dew-la)
Fern-leaf Yarrow

Mounds 3-5′ (0.9-1.5m). Foliage deeply cut, feathery. Flowers in summer; flat, yellow clusters 5″ (13cm) across. Space 24″ (60cm) apart.
Cultivars:
   'Gold Plate': deep yellow; height to 5′ (1.5m).
   'Parker's Variety': golden-yellow; height 3-4′ (0.9-1.2m).

Achillea millefolium

Achillea tomentosa

Achillea ptarmica

Achillea × 'Moonshine'

ACHILLEA (cont'd)

A. millefolium (mil-ee-FOH-li-um) N
Common Yarrow
Rapid spreader with mat-like habit, 12-24″ (30-60cm) tall. Dark green, deeply cut foliage. Flowers from mid-summer to early fall; colors vary white to red, in larger individual florets than those of the yellow-flowered yarrows. Naturalized. Space about 15″ (38cm) apart. Cultivars:
   'Rosea': rose-pink; height to 20″ (50cm).
   'Red Beauty': crimson-red; height 18″ (45cm).

A. ptarmica (TAR-mi-ka) N
Sneezewort
Vigorously spreading plant growing 12-24″ (30-60cm) high. Dark green willow-like finely-toothed leaves. White, ball-shaped flower clusters in early summer. Space 12-15″ (30-38cm) apart. A true native.

A. tomentosa (toh-men-TOH-sa) ⌇ N
Woolly Yarrow
Low-growing spreader mounds 6-12″ (15-30cm) high. Good rock garden plant. Grows vigorously in ideal conditions. Light grayish-green, hairy foliage. Sulfur-yellow flowers in early summer; cut flowers dry well. Naturalized. Space 12-15″ (30-38cm) apart.

A. × 'Moonshine'
Moonshine Yarrow
Less aggressive hybrid has deeply cut, silvery-gray foliage. Sulfur-yellow flowers in summer on 24″ (60cm) plants. Provide excellent drainage for best results. Space about 12″ (30cm) apart.

A. Galaxy Hybrids
Larger flowers and stronger stems resulted from a cross between A. millefolium and A. taygetea. Foliage similar to that of A. millefolium. Height to 36″ (90cm). Space 12-18″ (30-45cm) apart. Cultivars:
   'Appleblossom': clear peach-pink flowers.
   'Beacon': crimson-red blossoms have yellow centers.
   'Great Expectations': sandstone yellow flowers on shorter plant; grows to 24″ (60cm).
   'Salmon Beauty': large, light salmon-pink flowers.

23

Aconitum napellus

Mixed Perennial Garden

ACONITUM (a-ko-NY-tum) ○ ◑ ✂
Monkshood

Showy plants mound 3-6′(0.9-1.8m). Prefers rich, moist soil; healthy, established plants best left undisturbed. Attractive dark green deeply divided leaves. Blue flowers in spikes or clusters in late summer.

Note: all plant parts are poisonous; when cutting, avoid infecting open wounds.

Zones: 3-8
Spacing: 12-18″ (30-45cm)
Propagation: division of tuberous roots; seed (slow to germinate)

A. ✕bicolor (BY-ku-lor)
Bicolor Monkshood
Clusters of blue-edged white flowers in late summer and fall. Height 3-4′ (0.9-1.2m).

A. carmichaelii (kar-mi-KAY-lee-y)
Azure Monkshood
Foliage thick and leathery. Spikes of deep blue flowers in late summer, early fall. Height 3-5′ (0.9-1.5m).

A. napellus (na-PEL-lus)
Common Monkshood, Aconite Monkshood
Late summer flowers are dark blue. Height 3-4′ (0.9-1.2m).

ADENOPHORA (a-de-NOF-o-ra) ○ ◑   Not illustrated
Ladybells

Dainty plant looks somewhat like Canterbury Bells, though with more slender and branching stems. Needs well-drained soil; best left undisturbed. Leaves hug stems. Summer flowers are shades of blue, nodding and bell-shaped, borne in spikes.

Zones: 2-8
Spacing: 18-24″ (45-60cm)
Propagation: seed

A. confusa (kon-FEW-sa)
Common Ladybells
Deep blue flowers, each about ¾″ (2cm) long. Height 24-36″ (60-90cm).

A. liliifolia (li-lee-i-FOH-li-a)
Lilyleaf Ladybells
Pale blue flowers are ½″ (1.3cm) long. Height to 24″ (60cm).

Aegopodium podograria 'Variegatum'

Aethionema ✕ *warleyense*

Adonis amurensis

ADONIS (a-DOH-nis) ○ ◑

Low-growing perennials effective in rock garden or massed at front of border. Light green, feathery foliage. Large, clear yellow, cup-shaped flowers on erect stems, from early spring to early summer. Annual Adonis adds reds and coppery tones. Best in well-drained sandy loam.

Zones: 3-7
Spacing: 6-10″ (15-25cm)
Propagation: seed, division

A. amurensis (a-moo-REN-sis)
Amur Adonis
Height 9-12″ (23-30cm). Starts flowering very early, as soon as frost is out of ground; yellow flowers are 2-3″ (5-8cm) across, often more than one per stem. Foliage dies back in early summer. Tolerates dry soil.

A. vernalis (ver-NAH-lis)
Spring Adonis
Height 12-15″ (30-38cm). Buttercup-yellow flowers from early spring, one per stem. Foliage persists until early fall.

AEGOPODIUM (ee-goh-POH-di-um) ○ ◑ ● ⤳ N
Bishop's Weed
A. podograria 'Variegatum' (poh-doh-GRAH-ri-a ve-ri-e-GAH-tum)
Silveredge Bishop's Weed, Goutweed, Snow-on-the-mountain
Versatile, fast-spreading groundcover that grows 6-12″ (15-30cm) high. Useful where little else will grow, in sun or shade, rich or poor soil. Leaves green with silver margins. Insignificant white flowers in mid-summer; remove to prevent self-seeding. May become invasive. Naturalized. Tolerates extra-moist soils.

Zones: 3-10
Spacing: 10-15″ (25-38cm)
Propagation: division in spring or fall

AETHIONEMA (ee-thi-oh-NEE-ma) ○ ♠
Stonecress
A. ✕ warleyense (war-lay-EN-see) [*A. grandiflorum* 'Warley Rose']
Warley Rose Stonecress
Low-growing shrubby evergreen grows 6-8″ (15-20cm) high. Prefers light, sandy soil. Good in rock gardens and as edging or small area groundcover. Blue-green foliage. Flowers bright pink in spring. Shear back lightly after flowering to encourage fresh new growth.

Zones: 6-9
Spacing: 12-15″ (30-38cm)
Propagation: seed, cuttings, division

Ajuga genevensis

Alcea rosea

Ajuga reptans 'Burgundy Glow'

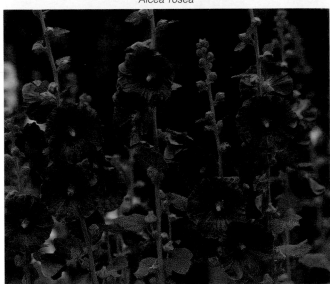

Alcea rosea

AJUGA (a-JOO-ga) ○ ◑ ⤳ ♠
Bugleweed

Low, fast-growing groundcover. Thrives in almost any well-drained soil. Leaves form dense mat or mound. Full sun enhances foliage colors. Flowers from late spring to early summer.

Zones: 3-9
Spacing: 6-12″ (15-30cm)
Propagation: division, seed

A. genevensis (je-ne-VEN-sis)
Geneva Bugleweed

Forms clumps 6-9″ (15-23cm). Dark green, toothed leaves. Flower spikes 2″ (5cm) long, bright blue, pink or white. Good for rock gardens.

A. pyramidalis (pi-ra-mi-DAH-lis)
Upright Bugleweed

Forms clumps 6-9″ (15-23cm) tall. Dark foliage is smoother than that of *A. genevensis*. Blue flowers, in 4-6″ (10-15cm) spikes.

A. reptans (REP-tanz)
Carpet Bugle

Very low-growing, spreads rapidly by means of stolons (stems); height 4-12″ (10-30cm). Leaf color variable, flowers blue or purple.

A. reptans cultivars:
'Burgundy Glow': foliage shades of white, pink, rose, and green turn deep bronze in fall; younger leaves have rosy hue.
'Gaiety': bronze-purple leaves; lilac flowers.
'Pink Beauty': flowers deep pink, in spikes 4-5″ (10-13cm) long.
'Silver Beauty': gray-green leaves are edged white.

ALCEA (al-SEE-a) ○ ✄
A. rosea (ROH-zee-a)
Garden Hollyhock

Biennials or shortlived perennials. Usually reseed spontaneously. Plant at back or center of border, or grow against fence or wall. Bright green leaves are felt-like and hairy. Flower spikes can rise 5-9′ (1.5-2.7m). Individual blossoms 3-5″ (8-13cm) across; single, ruffled, frilled, or double blooms in nearly every shade of white, pink, yellow and lavender. Best in moist though well-drained soil, with good air circulation.
Cultivars:
'Chater's Double': scarlet, pink, white and yellow double flowers are ruffled and ball-shaped. Height 4-6′ (1.2-1.8m).
'Powderpuffs': large double flowers on spikes 4-5′ (1.2-1.5m) tall; colors are yellow, white, pink, scarlet and salmon.

Zones: 3-8
Spacing: 15-18″ (38-45cm)
Propagation: seed

Alchemilla mollis

Allium schoenoprasum

ALCHEMILLA (al-ke-MIL-a) ◑

Lady's-mantle

Low-growing perennial for shady areas. Large rounded or lobed leaves are grayish light green. Flowers in spring; green or yellow clusters of petal-less blossoms readily scatter seed that can extend the planting. Needs consistent soil moisture.

Zones: 3-10
Spacing: 10-12″ (25-30cm)
Propagation: seed, division

A. alpina (al-PY-na)
Mountain Lady's-mantle
Dwarf habit, good for groundcover in no-traffic areas. Height 6-8″ (15-20cm). Deeply cut 2″ (5cm) green leaves have silvery margins.

A. mollis (MOL-is) ✂
Common Lady's-mantle
Height 12-18″ (30-45cm). Leaves have shallow lobes. Flowers in early summer, with chartreuse-colored starry clusters.

ALLIUM (AL-i-um) ○ ◑

Ornamental Onion

Decorative relatives of the onion, useful in border or rock garden and as edging plants. Best in full sun, planted to depth of three times bulb diameter, in well-drained soil. Foliage dies back during or after blooming. Typical onion smell given off only when plant tissues are cut or crushed.

Zones: 4-9
Spacing: varies with size of species
Propagation: seed, division

A. sativum (sa-TEE-vum)
Garlic
Height to 24″ (60cm), leaves about 1″ (2.5cm) wide, flowers pinkish. Bulblets (cloves) used for flavoring. Often grown as annual when all bulbs are lifted each summer or fall.

A. schoenoprasum (shoh-noh-PRAY-sum)
Chives
Useful edging or mid-border species, 24″ (60cm) tall. Gray-green leaves are tasty when cut into salads and for cooking. Rose-purple flower clusters in summer. Space 4-6″ (10-15cm) apart. Spreads rapidly in rich, moist soil. Plant at soil level.

Amsonia tabernaemontana

Anchusa azurea

Anaphalis triplinervis

Antennaria dioica

AMSONIA (am-SOH-ni-a) ◑ N
Bluestar
A. tabernaemontana (ta-ber-nee-mon-TAH-na)
Willow Amsonia
Low maintenance perennial for borders and natural plantings. Height about 3½′ (1.05m). Grows well in moist, cool places; tolerates dry soil, full sun with reduced vigor. Willow-like leaves are gray-green. Flowers steel blue, borne in terminal clusters in late spring.
Zones: 3-9
Spacing: 15-18″ (38-45cm)
Propagation: seed, division in spring or fall

ANAPHALIS (a-NAF-a-lis) ○ ✂
A. triplinervis (tri-pli-NER-vis)
Pearly Everlasting
Compact, easy gray-green plant mounds 12-18″ (30-45cm). Best in evenly moist soil. Good for naturalizing; tolerates drought, partial shade. Leaves have dense white furry covering. Masses of small white flowers from summer until frost. Excellent for cutting and drying.
Zones: 3-8
Spacing: 12-15″ (30-38cm)
Propagation: division, seed

ANCHUSA (an-KOO-sa) ○
Alkanet, Bugloss
A. azurea (a-ZEW-ree-a)
Italian Bugloss
Short lived, selfseeding perennials with crisp blue flowers. Height 3-5′ (0.9-1.5m); grows well in any soil except in wet conditions. Will tolerate some shade. Loosely structured plants may require support. Leaves hairy, 4-8″ (10-20cm) long. Flowers bright blue, in one-sided clusters. Colorful filler plants among more formal perennials.
Cultivars:
  'Little John': compact habit, height to 18″ (45cm) dark blue flowers.
  'Loddon Royalist': gentian-blue flowers on 36″ (90cm) plants.

Zones: 3-10
Spacing: 18-24″ (45-60cm)
Propagation: division, root cuttings, seed

When planting near a wall or building, remember to leave space for air circulation behind the plants. A three-foot (ninety centimeter) or greater gap allows access behind young plants for weeding and cultivation, and protects them from excessive buildup of reflected heat.

Anemone hupehensis var. japonica

Anemone hupehensis var. japonica

Anemone vitifolia

ANEMONE (a-NEM-oh-nee) ◗✂
Anemone, Windflower
Showy plants with a variety of different forms and colors. Compound or divided leaves, and petal-less flowers. Color is provided by showy sepals. Grow in any well-drained soil. Shelter from afternoon sun.
Zones: 5-10
Spacing: varies by species
Propagation: division, root cuttings, seed

A. canadensis (ka-na-DEN-sis) N
Meadow Anemone
White flowers top plants in summer. Light green, segmented foliage contrasts well with darker shrubs, evergreens. Height 24″ (60cm). Space 12″ (30cm) apart. Hardy to zone 3.

A. hupehensis var. japonica (hew-pe-HEN-sis ja-PON-i-ka)
Japanese Anemone
and **A. ✕hybrida** (HYB-ri-da)
Windflower
Late summer flowers may be pink or white, single or double. Foliage light green. Height 30-36″ (75-90cm). Space 18″ (45cm) apart.

A. sylvestris (sil-VES-tris)
Snowdrop Anemone
White spring flowers followed by fluffy white fruits. Foliage light green. Height 10-18″ (25-45cm). Best in partial shade. Space 12″ (30cm) apart.

A. vitifolia (vi-ti-FOH-li-a)
Grape-leaf Anemone
Fall blooming anemone has dark green lobed leaves and white flowers. Stoloniferous plants form clumps 18-36″ (45-90cm) high. Space 18″ (45cm) apart.

ANTENNARIA (an-te-NAH-ri-a) ○ ⋙
Pussy-toes, Cat's-ears
A. dioica (dy-OH-i-ka)
Common Pussy-toes
Rapidly spreading mat of 1″ (2.5cm) gray-green or silver leaves. Tolerates poor soil and dry conditions. Useful as a quick filler; contain spread by dividing plants. Pinkish tips on light green flower clusters resemble cat's toes. Flowers in late spring.
A. dioica var. rosea (ROH-zee-a): rose-red flowers on stems 8-10″ (20-25cm) high.
Cultivar **'Tomentosa'** [A. tomentosa (toh-men-TOH-sa)]: creamy white flower clusters rise only to 3″ (8cm).
Zones: 3-8
Spacing: 10-12″ (25-30cm)
Propagation: division in spring, seed

Anthemis species

Aquilegia in mixed perennial planting

ANTHEMIS (AN-the-mis) ○ ✕ ♠
Golden Marguerite

Showy mounds with bright yellow, orange or white daisies and aromatic, finely divided foliage. Tolerates poor soil; excessive fertilizer may result in unsightly growth. Useful for cutting during summer; trim off old flowers to encourage fresh blossoms.

Zones: vary by species
Spacing: 12-24″ (30-60cm)
Propagation: division every 2-3 years, seed

A. marschalliana (mar-shal-ee-AH-na)
[*A. biebersteiniana* (bee-ber-sty-nee-AH-na)]
Marshall Chamomile

Golden-yellow flowers top silvery foliage. Smaller than many *Anthemis* species: height 12-18″ (30-45cm). Useful in rock gardens. Zones 5-7.

A. tinctoria (tink-TOH-ri-a)
Golden Marguerite

Excellent border plant. Mounds 24-36″ (60-90cm) high; may need staking in rich soils. Flowers yellow, about 1½″ (4cm) across. Cut back hard after flowering to encourage new growth. Zones 3-9.
Cultivars:

'E.C. Buxton': flowers off-white with lemon-yellow centers; height to 30″ (75cm).

'Kelwayi': bright golden-yellow flowers.

AQUILEGIA (ak-wi-LEE-ji-a) ○ ◐ ✕
Columbine

Attractive mounds of airy fan-like or ferny leaves with long-stemmed pastel flowers. Best with good moisture supply in well-drained, rich soil. Needs partial shade in hot dry areas. Dainty multi-colored blossoms attract hummingbirds in spring and early summer. Mulch plants in zones 3-5 from late fall to early spring to prevent heaving as soil freezes and thaws.

Zones: 3-10
Spacing: 10-15″ (25-38cm)
Propagation: seed

A. caerulea (se-REW-lee-a) **N**
American, Blue, or Colorado Columbine

Blue-purple or white flowers in early summer. Height 18-36″ (45-90cm).

A. canadensis (ka-na-DEN-sis) **N**
Wild Columbine

Early spring red-and-yellow blossoms on 12-36″ (30-90cm) plants. Best in moist, shady locations.

A. chrysantha (kri-SAN-tha) **N**
Golden Columbine

Spring flowers are yellow. Height 30-42″ (75-100cm). Plants may need staking for support.

Aquilegia canadensis

Arabis caucasica

Aquilegia × hybrida

AQUILEGIA (cont'd)

A. flabellata (fla-be-LAH-ta)
Fan Columbine
Shorter plant with white or pink-tinged flowers. Useful for border front and rock garden. Grows 8-18″ (20-45cm) tall. Leaf segments often overlap and are darker green than those of other columbines.

A. formosa (for-MOH-sa) **N**
Sitka, Red, Western, or California Columbine
Red and yellow flowers from early summer. Height about 36″ (90cm).

A. × hybrida
Hybrid Columbine
Blooms in early summer; large, upright flowers in wide range of colors.
Cultivars:
  'Biedermeier' (Nosegay Columbine): compact plants 9-12″ (23-30cm) tall; flowers mostly blue and white.
  'Dragon Fly': mixed colors; height 18-24″ (45-60cm).
  'Music': many colors available; height 18-20″ (45-50cm).
  'Nora Barlow': fully double flowers look like small dahlias; color reddish pink, edged white; height 24-30″ (60-75cm).

ARABIS (AR-a-bis) ○ ⚘ ▲
Rock Cress
Low, spreading evergreen perennial prefers cooler climates. Best in well-drained soil. Good edging, rock garden plant. Flowers white or pink.
Zones: 3-7
Spacing: 12-15″ (30-38cm)
Propagation: division, cuttings, seed

A. blepharophylla (ble-fa-roh-FIL-a) **N**
Rock Cress
Flat rosettes of dark green leaves. Fragrant, rose-purple flowers in spring. Mounds to 12″ (30cm). Give winter protection in northern zones. Cultivar **'Spring Charm'** has rose-tinted flowers.

A. caucasica (kaw-KAS-i-ka) [*A. albida* (AL-bi-da)]
Wall Rock Cress
Spreading plant forms loose mat with succulent, whitish-green leaves and prolific white flowers in spring. Excellent on walls, in rock gardens. Height 8-10″ (20-25cm). Cut back hard after flowering to encourage thicker new growth. To renew clumps, divide vigorous plants every 2-3 years.
Cultivars:
  'Snow Cap': large white ornamental blossoms.
  'Flore Pleno': double white flowers; height to 12″ (30cm).

Arenaria montana

Arisaema triphyllum

Armeria maritima

ARENARIA (a-re-NAH-ri-a) ○ ◑ ⌇ ♠
Sandwort
Forms low, trailing mat of dense foliage. Prolific white flowers in early summer. Excellent for rock gardens.
Zones: 4-9
Spacing: 10-12″ (25-30cm)
Propagation: seed, division, cuttings

A. montana (mon-TAH-na)
Mountain Sandwort
Glossy green leaves and big 1″ (2.5cm) white flowers. Best in slightly acid soil. Tolerates moist soils. Height 2-4″ (5-10cm).

A. verna (VER-na)
[*A. caespitosa* (sez-pi-TOH-sa)]
Moss Sandwort
Fine, moss-like evergreen leaves. Grows rapidly in sun or part shade. Late spring flowers are white, star-like, ½″ (1.3cm) across.

Rake fallen leaves or shred them to prevent lawn and other groundcover plants from being stifled by a blanket of damp or frozen leaves.

ARISAEMA (a-ris-EE-ma) ○ ◑ N
A. triphyllum (tri-FIL-um)
Jack-in-the-pulpit
Tuberous perennial with large green to purple spathe or sheath surrounding flower spike (spadix). Prefers fertile, moist yet well-drained soil. Height 16-20″ (40-50cm). Leaves three-lobed. Flowers in summer; bright red berries in fall. **Note: all plant parts are poisonous.**
Zones: 4-9
Spacing: 12-18″ (30-45cm)
Propagation: seed, division

ARMERIA (ar-MEE-ri-a) ○ ⌇ ♠
Thrift, Sea Pink
A. maritima (ma-RIT-i-ma)
Common Thrift
Tufts of blue-green narrow leaves form spreading clumps that mound to 6-12″ (15-30cm). Tolerates seaside garden conditions. Best in light, sandy, well-drained soil. Good for rock garden, edging, or front of border. Flowers in summer; masses of ball-shaped clusters of pink, mauve-red, lilac, or white blossoms rise above foliage. Plants benefit from afternoon shade in southern gardens.
Zones: 3-9
Spacing: 9-12″ (23-30cm)
Propagation: division, seed

Arrhenatherum elatius var. *bulbosum* 'Variegatum'

Artemisia dracunculus

Artemisia absinthium

Artemesia lactiflora

ARRHENATHERUM (a-re-NATH-e-rum) ○ ◑ ✹ N
A. elatius* var. *bulbosum (e-LAH-ti-us bul-BOH-sum)
Tuber Oat Grass
Oat-like grass with broad, cascading leaf-blades about 12″ (30cm) long. Clumps mound to 2-4′ (0.6-1.2m). Purplish-green flower clusters are narrow on tall stems. Tuberous roots. Thrives in any fertile soil; tolerates drought when established. Grows best with cooler spring and fall temperatures. Naturalized.
Cultivar **'Variegatum'** has ivory leaf margins.
Zones: 3-10
Spacing: 15″ (38cm)
Propagation: division

ARTEMISIA (ar-te-MIZ-i-a) ○ ◑
Wormwood
Useful edging and border plants with silvery, fern-like, aromatic foliage that may persist through winter. Thrive in poor, dry soils. Good in dry, sunny climates and where winter conditions remain dry. Excess moisture can cause rotting, and over-fertilization results in unsightly growth. Flowers usually inconspicuous.
Zones: 3-9: see individual species
Spacing: 12-15″ (30-38cm)
Propagation: division, cuttings, seed

A. absinthium (ab-SIN-thi-um) **N**
Common Wormwood, Absinthe
Silvery-gray, finely divided foliage mounds 24-36″ (60-90cm). Tiny gray flowers in late summer. Dried leaves sometimes used medicinally. Naturalized.
Cultivars and hybrids:
  'Lambrook Silver': good accent 30″ (75cm) high; cut back in summer to encourage dense new growth.
  ***A.* ✕ 'Powis Castle':** fine textured, vigorous evergreen; grows 36″ (90cm) high.

A. dracunculus (dra-KUN-kew-lus)
Tarragon
Upright gray-green herb useful as background for lower-growing plants and as source of culinary tarragon. Height 18″ (45cm). Zones 5-9.
A. d.* var. *sativa (sa-TY-va), **French Tarragon,** has flavorful leaves used in cooking and in perfumery.

A. lactiflora (lak-ti-FLOH-ra) ✂
White Mugwort
Creamy-white flowers appear in late summer, in big, long-lasting plume-like clusters. Green foliage is lobed and toothed, provides good foil for flowers planted in front. Height 4-6′ (1.2-1.8m). Tolerates partial shade. Zones 5-8.

Artemisia ludoviciana 'Silver King'

Artemisia schmidtiana

Aruncus dioicus

ARTEMISIA (cont'd)

A. ludoviciana (loo-doh-vik-ee-AH-na) N
White Sage

Compact plant with 2-4″ (5-10cm) silvery-gray leaves on whitish stems. Late summer flowers are gray. Height 2-4′ (0.6-1.2m).
Cultivars:

'Silver King': deep silver leaves; flower plumes show unusual red color in fall.

'Silver Queen': silvery foliage has deeply cut margins.

A. schmidtiana (schmit-ee-AH-na) ⚘
Satiny Wormwood, Silver Mound Artemisia

Mounding intense silver-gray plant with satiny, finely cut leaves. Height 15-24″ (38-60cm). Summer flowers small and yellow. Best when trimmed before flowers fully develop to maintain mound form. Usually available in compact forms known as **'Nana'** or **'Silver Mound'** with height of 6-12″ (15-30cm).

ARUNCUS (a-RUN-kus) ○ ◐
Goatsbeard

Stately, shrub-like perennials that produce creamy-white plumes of blossoms in early summer. Forms large yet non-invasive clumps in rich soil. Best with shade and moisture in southern areas, full sun in north. Leaves compound. Male and female flowers on different plants.
Zones: 4-9
Spacing: 3-5′ (0.98-1.5m); smaller selections 18-24″ (45-60cm)
Propagation: division, seed

A. aethusifolius (ee-thoo-si-FOH-li-us)
Miniature Goatsbeard

True miniature, growing to just 8-12″ (20-30cm). Good for rock garden, front of border. Tolerates partial shade. Leaves deeply cut.

A. dioicus (dy-OH-i-kus) N
[A. sylvester (sil-VES-ter)]
Goatsbeard

Flower plumes rise 4-6′ (1.2-1.8m) in late spring. Leaves 24-36″ (60-90cm) long. Cultivar **'Kneiffii'** grows only 24-36″ (60-90cm) tall, has finely dissected compound leaves; space more closely.

Asarum europeaum

Asclepias tuberosa

ASARUM (a-SAH-rum) ●⤳
Wild Ginger
Rhizomatous perennials with fleshy, sometimes evergreen leaves that shelter pitcher-shaped flowers. Need rich, moist yet well-drained soil. Useful groundcover in damp, shaded area.
Zones: vary by species
Spacing: 6-10″ (15-25cm)
Propagation: division, seed

A. canadense (ka-na-DEN-see) N
Wild Ginger, Snakeroot
Heart-shaped leaves are about 6″ (15cm) wide. Height 4-6″ (10-15cm). Zones 3-7.

A. europaeum (ew-roh-PAY-um)
European Wild Ginger
Dark green, glossy evergreen leaves 2-3″ (5-8cm) wide. Height 4-6″ (10-15cm). Zones 4-7.

A. shuttleworthii (shu-tel-WOR-thee-y) ♠ N
Mottled or Southern Wild Ginger
Leaves broad, often silvery-mottled. Height about 8″ (20cm). Zones 6-10.

A. virginicum (vir-JIN-i-kum) ♠ N
Virginia Wild Ginger
Green-leaved wild ginger grows to about 7″ (17.5cm). Zones 5-10.

ASCLEPIAS (as-KLEE-pi-as) ○ ✂ N
A. tuberosa (tew-be-ROH-sa)
Milkweed, Butterfly Flower
Upright and vigorous, tuberous-rooted perennial with narrow foliage. Best in well-drained sandy, fertile soil. Showy bright orange flowers in summer, followed by pointed seedpods; both flowers and seedpods useful for cut arrangements.
Zones: 4-9
Spacing: 10-12″ (20-30cm)
Propagation: seed, division

Aster alpinus

Aster × frikartii

Aster novi-belgii

ASTER (AS-ter) ○ ✕

Mounding or open habit perennials with colorful, yellow-centered daisy flowers. Best in well-drained soil. Heights range from 6″ (15cm) to 6′ (1.8m). Taller asters usually require staking for support. Encourage branching by pinching new growth in spring and early summer.

Zones: 3-8
Spacing: 12-24″ (30-60cm)
Propagation: division, cuttings, seed (species)

A. alpinus (al-PY-nus) **N**
Alpine Aster

Summer-flowering rock garden, front or edging plant for cooler areas. Flowers purple. Height 6-9″ (15-23cm). Gray-green foliage turns green in summer.

Cultivar **'Goliath'** has light blue flowers and grows to 15″ (38cm).

A. ✕frikartii (fri-KAR-tee-y)
Frikart's Aster

Lavender blossoms in summer. Plants grow 24-36″ (60-90cm). Dark green foliage is mildew-resistant.

Cultivar **'Mönch':** sturdy plant spreading about 36″ (90cm).

A. novae-angliae (NOH-vay-AN-glee-ay) **N**
New England Aster

Many cultivars available, with wide color range. Much-branched plants grow 4-6′ (1.2-1.8m) tall. Flower in late summer; species has violet-purple blossoms, 1½-2″ (4-5cm) across. Good for cutting.

A. novi-belgii (NOH-vee-BEL-jee-y) **N**
Michaelmas Daisy, New York Aster

Many cultivars with 1″ (2.5cm) blossoms in shades of lilac, blue, pink, red. Species is violet. Flower in late summer; good for cutting. Small or dwarf varieties grow to 15″ (38cm); medium varieties grow to 4′ (1.2m); and tall varieties grow to 6′ (1.8m).

A. tongolensis (ton-go-LEN-sis)
East Indies Aster

Short, vigorously spreading species produces 2″ (5cm) flowers in summer on strong stems that need no support. Flowers are violet-blue with bright orange centers. Divide plants after flowering to maintain vigor.

Astilbe × arendsii

Astilbe simplicifolia

Astilbe chinensis 'Pumila'

Astilbe taquetii

ASTILBE (a-STIL-bee)

Summer-flowering perennials that thrive in shady, moist locations. Best in deep, rich soil with good moisture and fertilizer supply. White, pink, red, or purple flower clusters rise in fluffy plumes over mounded green foliage. Leaves may have coppery color when young. Flowers good for cutting: harvest when half open, for use fresh or to dry for winter decoration. Intolerant of drought while growing, and too much moisture in winter.

Zones: 4-9
Spacing: 12-18″ (30-45cm)
Propagation: division

A. × arendsii (a-REND-zee-y)
Astilbe, False Spirea
Many cultivars flowering in mid- to late summer, with colors that range from clear white to blood red. Foliage colors from copper to dark green. Height 2-4′ (0.6-1.2m). Best in moist but not soggy soil.
Cultivars:
  'Etna': dark red; mid-summer; height 24″ (60cm).
  'Fanal': dark blood red; mid-summer; leaves dark bronze; height 24″ (60cm).
  'Deutschland': white; early summer; height 24″ (60cm).
  'Rheinland': delicate pink; early summer; height 24″ (60cm)

A. chinensis (chi-NEN-sis)
Chinese Astilbe
Rosy-purple flowers in summer, on 18-36″ (45-90cm) plants. Foliage deeply cut, bronze-green. Somewhat drought tolerant.
Cultivar **'Pumila'** grows only 8-12″ (20-30cm) and is good for rock gardens and front of borders.

A. simplicifolia (sim-pli-si-FOH-li-a)
Star Astilbe
White, star-like flowers on dwarf 12-18″ (30-45cm) plants. Forms compact mounds. Leaves not divided.
Cultivar **'Sprite'** has airy shell-pink flowers followed by attractive rust-colored fruits.

A. taquetii (tar-KET-ee-y)
Fall Astilbe
Late summer flowering astilbe with excellent vase life when cut. Lilac colored blossoms followed by attractive fruits that remain all winter. Height 2-4′ (0.6-1.2m).
Cultivar **'Superba'** blooms into early fall. Flowers magenta or red-purple. Foliage bronze-green.

Athyrium filix-femina

Aubrieta deltoidea

Aurinia saxatilis

ATHYRIUM (a-THI-ri-um) ● N
A. filix-femina (FIL-iks-FEM-i-na)
Lady Fern
Deciduous fern with arching pale green fronds. Needs moist, humus-rich soil. Height 2-4′ (0.6-1.2m). Tolerates some sun.
Zones: 4-9
Spacing: 12-24″ (30-60cm)
Propagation: division, spores

AUBRIETA (aw-bree-AY-ta) ○ ◑ ᕤ ♠
A. deltoidea (del-TOI-dee-a)
Rock Cress
Compact, spreading perennials for rock gardens, edging, and front of borders. Mounds 6-8″ (15-20cm). Best in well-drained soil, in full sun except in hot areas. Flowers red to lilac, from spring to early summer. Cut back after flowering to encourage dense new growth.
Zones: 4-9
Spacing: 15-18″ (38-45cm)
Propagation: seed, division, cuttings

AURINIA (aw-RIN-i-a) ○ ◑ ᕤ
A. saxatilis (sak-SAT-i-lis)
[*Alyssum saxatile* (a-LIS-um sak-SAT-i-lee)]
Basket-of-gold
Fast-growing rock garden, wall, or front of border plant thrives in full sun. Mounds 6-12″ (15-30cm). Gray-green foliage. Brilliant yellow flowers in tight clusters, from early spring to early summer. Trim to shape after flowering.
Cultivars:
  'Citrinum': mounds 10-15″ (25-38cm); lemon-yellow flowers.
  'Compactum': compact plants grow 8-10″ (20-25cm); bright golden-yellow flowers.

Zones: 3-7
Spacing: 12″ (30cm)
Propagation: softwood cuttings, division, seed

Baptisia australis

Bellis perennis

BAPTISIA (bap-TIZ-i-a) ○ ◐ **N**
False Indigo, Wild Indigo
Bushy plants grow 3-5′ (0.9-1.5m) tall. Best in deep rich, neutral to acid soil, with good moisture supply: will tolerate poorer soils. Among the earliest perennials to grow in early spring. Leaflets in threes, rich bluish-green. Loose clusters of pea-like flowers.

Zones: 3-10
Spacing: 18-24″ (45-60cm)
Propagation: seed, division

B. australis (aw-STRAH-lis) ✄
Blue False Indigo
Blue flowers in early summer. Bushy plants form seasonal hedge or screen.

B. tinctoria (tink-TOH-ri-a)
Yellow False Indigo, Horsefly Weed
Yellow flowers in summer. Tolerates neglect and periods of drought. Good for natural plantings.

BELLIS (BEL-is) ○
B. perennis (pe-REN-nis)
English Daisy
Tender perennial, treated as a biennial or annual in northern zones. Needs well-drained soil. Good for edging and in rock gardens. Dark green leaves in 6″ (15cm) clumps. Flowers in early spring; white, pink, or red daisies are 1-2″ (2.5-5cm) across. Remove dead flowers regularly to encourage more bloom. In zones 3-5, lift plants and hold through winter under straw in cold frame. Elsewhere, lift and divide plants every two years to maintain vigor.

Zones: 6-10
Spacing: 8-10″ (20-25cm)
Propagation: seed, division

Small perennial groups are easier to position for an attractive cluster when odd numbers of plants (3, 5, 7, or 9) are used rather than even numbers. Larger, massed plantings will absorb any number.

Boltonia asteroides

Bergenia cordifolia

Brunnera macrophylla

BERGENIA (ber-GEN-i-a) ◯ ◐ ᵚᵚ ♠ ✕
B. cordifolia (kor-di-FOH-li-a)
Heartleaf Bergenia

Vigorous, spreading, large-leaved perennial makes good groundcover, border, or rock garden plant. Foliage grows 10″ (25cm) across, glossy green turning deep burgundy in cold weather. Grows in any good garden soil; tolerates moisture. Early spring flowers rise in showy clusters. Plants mound 12-18″ (30-45cm).
Cultivars:

'Bressingham White': pink-colored blooms become pure white as they open and mature.
'Morning Red': dark purplish-red flowers; bronze-green foliage; lower growing mound, 8-12″ (20-30cm) high.
'Perfecta': lilac-red flowers and big pale purplish-brown foliage.
'Silver Light': white flowers become pink; foliage shiny, dark green.

Zones: 4-10
Spacing: 12-15″ (30-45cm)
Propagation: seed, division in spring

BOLTONIA (bol-TOH-ni-a) ◯ **N**
B. asteroides (as-te-ROI-deez)
White Boltonia

Tall, informal, aster-like plant, for back of borders, natural gardens. Thrives in any good garden soil; spreads rapidly in moist conditions. Vigorous plants 5-7′ (1.5-2.1m) tall; may need staking. Blue-green leaves. Showy clusters of white or purple daisies in late summer. Cultivar **'Snowbank'** has white flowers, tolerates heat and humidity, grows to 3-4′ (0.9-1.2m). Rarely needs staking when grown in full sun.
Zones: 4-9
Spacing: 18-24″ (45-60cm)
Propagation: division, seed (species)

BRUNNERA (BROO-ne-ra) ◯ ◐ ●
B. macrophylla (mak-roh-FIL-a)
Heartleaf Brunnera

Fast growing perennial does well in moist and shady locations. Mid-green, heart-shaped foliage mounds 12-18″ (30-45cm) high. Loose, branching clusters of light blue forget-me-not blossoms open in spring.
Zones: 3-9
Spacing: 12-15″ (30-38cm)
Propagation: seed, root cuttings, division

Calamagrostis ✕ acutiflora 'Stricta'

Caltha palustris

CALAMAGROSTIS (ka-la-ma-GROS-tis) ○ ✂ ⸶
Reed Grass
Vigorous, upright ornamental grasses with slender stems and rough-edged leaves. Flower from summer to fall. Thrive in any fertile soil. Tolerate moist conditions; good for waterside plantings. Cut flower plumes fresh or dried. Remove faded tops before new growth starts in spring.
Zones: 5-9
Spacing: 18-24″ (45-60cm)
Propagation: division

C. ✕ acutiflora **'Stricta'** (a-kew-ti-FLOH-ra STRIK-ta)
Feather Reed Grass
Robust and showy, height 3-5′ (0.9-1.5m). Flower plumes rise to 5′ (1.5m) or more in summer. Striking, wheat-colored seed heads persist into winter.

C. arundinacea **var.** *brachytricha*
(a-run-di-NAY-see-a bra-ki-TRIK-a)
Korean Reed Grass
Lower form with gracefully arching foliage. Height 24-36″ (60-90cm). Flowers in fall, shimmering white or pinkish plumes. Whole plant turns buff-colored after frost. Flower heads persist into winter.

CALTHA (KAL-tha) ○ **N**
C. palustris (pa-LUS-tris)
Marsh Marigold
Moisture-loving perennial for marshy areas and close to water. Height to 24″ (60cm). Best in rich, boggy soil. Shiny green leaves. Clear yellow single or double buttercup flowers in spring. Dies back in summer; tolerates dry soil when dormant. Tolerates some shade.
Zones: 4-9
Spacing: 12-24″ (30-60cm)
Propagation: seed, division

○ = Full Sun		♠ = Evergreen	
◑ = Partial Shade		**N** = Native or Naturalized Plant	
● = Shade		⸶ = Ornamental Grass	
〰 = Groundcover		✂ = Cut Flowers	

Campanula carpatica 'Blue Clips'

Campanula carpatica 'White Clips'

Campanula glomerata

CAMPANULA (kam-PAN-ew-la) ○ ◑
Bellflower

Perennial bellflowers range from low-growing rock garden plants to tall border plants useful for cut flowers. All prefer moist, well-drained garden soil; use baits to deter slugs and snails. Spring and/or summer flowers in white and shades of blue to pink; delicate colors develop best in partly shaded locations.

Zones: 4-10: see individual species
Spacing: 12-18″ (30-45cm)
Propagation: seed, division, cuttings

C. carpatica (kar-PAT-i-ka)
Carpathian or **Tussock Harebell**

Low spreader for rock garden and front of border. Height 6-12″ (15-30cm). Spreads rapidly in well-drained soil. Clumps of dark green foliage topped in summer by clusters of 1½-2″ (4-5cm) bright blue flowers. Mulch in warmer climates to keep roots cool.

Cultivars:
  'Blue Clips' and **'White Clips':** compact plants grow to 6-9″ (15-23cm) with big 3″ (8cm) violet-blue/white flowers, light green leaves.
  'China Doll': azure-blue flowers on 9″ (23cm) plants.
  'Wedgewood Blue' and **'Wedgewood White':** violet-blue/white flowers on compact 9″ (23cm) plants.

C. elatines var. *garganica* (EL-a-teenz gar-GAH-ni-ka)
Elatines Bellflower

(Offered as *C. garganica*)

Mat-forming rock garden and edging plants, 5-6″ (13-15cm) tall. Leaves grayish-green, kidney or heart-shaped. Flowers late spring to early summer, clusters of white-eyed, pale blue star-like blossoms. Hardy only as far north as zone 6.

C. glomerata (glo-me-RAH-ta) ✂
Clustered Bellflower

Blue, purple, or white clusters of flowers top 12-18″ (30-45cm) plants in summer. Stoloniferous, spreads quickly in good soils.

Cultivars:
  'Joan Elliott': more compact and branching, to 15-18″ (38-35cm); deep violet-blue flowers.
  'Superba' and **'Superba Alba':** vigorous plants grow 20-30″ (50-75cm) tall; big clusters of rich violet/white flowers; tolerates heat better than others.

Campanula persicifolia

Canna

Campanula persicifolia

Catananche caerulea

CAMPANULA (cont'd)

C. persicifolia (per-si-ki-FOH-li-a) ✂
Peachleaf Bellflower
Medium height, 12-36″ (30-90cm). Good for middle or back of border. Basal leaves evergreen in milder climates. Blue-violet flowers are broadly bell-shaped, borne in loose clusters. Remove faded flowers to extend summer flowering season.
Cultivars **'Alba'** (white) and **'Blue'** (sky-blue) both grow to about 30″ (75cm).

C. poscharskyana (po-shar-skee-AH-na)
Serbian Bellflower
Rapidly spreading, drought resistant bellflower for rock garden, dry wall, or edging. Blue-lilac flowers rise to 8-12″ (20-30cm) in spring. Prostrate stems, kidney-shaped leaves.

C. rotundifolia (roh-tun-di-FOH-li-a) **N**
Harebell, Bluebells-of-Scotland
Dainty, summer-flowering bellflower grows to 6-12″ (15-30cm). Tolerates cold climates. Basal leaves are rounded; foliage on flowering stems is slender, grass-like. Clear blue-violet flowers.
Cultivar **'Olympia'** has bright blue flowers and grows 12-18″ (30-45cm).

CANNA (KAN-a) ○
Canna Lily, Indian-shot
Tender perennials often planted each year in perennial or seasonal borders. Excellent for massed displays and in containers. Height 1½-5′ (0.45-1.5m). Broad, tropical-looking foliage may be bright green, bluish, or bronze. Flowers from mid-summer to fall, in showy colors that range from white to shades of yellow, orange, red, and pink. For overwintering in northern zones, lift rhizomes after frost has killed tops; store in moist peat moss at 40-45°F (5-10°C).
Zones: 7-10 (treat as annual in the North)
Spacing: 15-18″ (38-45cm)
Propagation: division

CATANANCHE (ka-ta-NAN-kee) ○ ✂
Cupid's-dart
C. caerulea (se-REW-lee-a)
Blue Cupid's-dart
Upright border perennial grows 18-30″ (45-75cm). Best in fertile, well-drained soil. Summer flowers on wiry stems above narrow, gray-green leaves. Good in fresh or dried arrangements. Cultivars offer white and shades of blue. Damp soil may result in winter kill.
Zones: 4-10
Spacing: 15-18″ (38-40cm)
Propagation: division in spring; root cuttings in fall

Centaurea dealbata

Centaurea montana

Centaurea macrocephala

CENTAUREA (sen-TAW-ree-a) ○ ✂
Knapweed, Cornflower
Perennial cornflowers grow best in well-drained soil. Good in borders and for cutting.
Zones: 3-8
Spacing: 12-18″ (30-45cm)
Propagation: division, seed

C. dealbata (dee-al-BAY-ta)
Persian Cornflower
Late spring flowering, grows 18-30″ (45-75cm) tall. Leaves coarsely cut, may grow to 24″ (60cm). Deeply fringed lavender flowers 2-3″ (5-8cm) across.

C. macrocephala (mak-roh-KEF-a-la)
Globe Centaurea
Flowers in summer on 3-4′ (0.9-1.2m) plants. Deep green leaves have wavy margins. Yellow, globe-like flowers, 3-4″ (8-10cm) across.

C. montana (mon-TAH-na)
Mountain Bluet
Early summer flowers on spreading plants, 18-24″ (45-60cm) tall. Best in alkaline soils. Foliage silvery when young. Flowers deep cornflower-blue.

CENTRANTHUS (sen-TRAN-thus) ○◑ ✂
C. ruber (ROO-ber)
Red Valerian
Vigorous, dependable perennial thrives in infertile, alkaline, well-drained soils. Height 18-36″ (45-90cm). Useful in borders and for cutting. Blue-green leaves. Showy clusters of small carmine-red fragrant flowers, late spring to summer; cultivars are white and shades of red and rose. Cutting stimulates continued flower production.
Zones: 4-9
Spacing: 12-15″ (30-38cm)
Propagation: seed, division

CERASTIUM (se-RAS-ti-um) ○ ∿ ▲
C. tomentosum (toh-men-TOH-sum)
Snow-in-summer
Useful creeper for rock gardens, walls, and edging. Spreads rapidly in northern zones; may burn out in southern heat. Needs excellent drainage. Silvery leaves form blanket mounding 6-8″ (15-20cm). Bright white, small yet showy flowers in late spring and early summer. Shear or trim off fading flowers to stimulate dense new growth. Fertilize sparingly to contain vigor.
Zones: 2-7
Spacing: 12-24″ (30-60cm)
Propagation: seed, division

Centranthus ruber

Ceratostigma plumbaginoides

Cerastium tomentosum

Chamaemelum nobile

CERATOSTIGMA (se-ra-toh-STIG-ma) ○ ◑ ⋎
C. plumbaginoides (plum-ba-ji-NOI-deez)
[*Plumbago larpentiae* (plum-BAH-goh lar-PEN-tee-ay)]
Leadwort

Vigorous spreading mounds of shiny leaves thrive in almost any well-drained garden soil. Useful as edging, groundcover, or rock garden plant. Height 8-12″ (20-30cm). Foliage opens late in spring, turns bronze-red in fall. Flowers deep gentian-blue, from late summer to early fall. Provide winter protection in northern zones.

Zones: 6-10
Spacing: 18-24″ (45-60cm)
Propagation: division in spring

CHAMAEMELUM (ka-mee-MAY-lum) ○ ⋎ ♠
C. nobile (NOH-bi-lee)
[*Anthemis nobilis* (AN-the-mis NOH-bi-lis)]
Roman Chamomile

Low evergreen groundcover or lawn substitute forms soft gray-green mat about 4″ (10cm) thick. Spreads rapidly in well-drained soils; tolerates drought. Flowers from late spring; white daisy-like blossoms rise to 12-14″ (30-35cm). Trim or mow off flowers to maintain groundcover. Blossoms used in tea; oil has flavoring and softening qualities. Cultivar **'Treneague'** does not flower and is less vigorous, needs less trimming and mowing.

Zones: 4-9
Spacing: 10-18″ (25-45cm)
Propagation: seed, division

Many border plants are grown for their foliage rather than flower beauty. For example, *Artemisia* species and varieties make more compact and bushy growth if flower buds are trimmed off. To contain height and encourage spread of late season flowering plants such as *Chrysanthemum*, pinch out the lead shoots during late spring and early summer.

Cheiranthus cheiri

Chelone lyonii

CHEIRANTHUS (kay-RAN-thus) ○ ◑
C. cheiri (KAY-ree)
English Wallflower

Short-lived perennial thrives in moist, temperate climates; best grown as biennial elsewhere. Late spring flowers are fragrant and showy in yellow, gold, red, and mahogany. Especially attractive when grouped or massed in borders, containers. Height 9-18″ (23-45cm).

Zones: 5-9

Spacing: 6-12″ (15-30cm)

Propagation: cuttings, seed. Sow seed in late summer for bloom next spring; maintain seedlings in protected area like cold frame; plant out in early spring after last hard freeze.

Once the spring sunlight is strong enough to warm the soil surface, remove winter mulches and prick or cultivate the top inch or two between herbaceous perennials and other plants. The first fertilizer may now be applied. At the same time, check for snails, slugs, and other pests, removing plant debris so new growth will not be infected or infested.

CHELONE (ke-LOH-nee) ◑ N
C. lyonii (ly-OH-nee-y)
Pink Turtlehead

Unusual perennial for moist, rich soils and wet areas. Best in acid conditions; tolerates some alkalinity. Height 24-36″ (60-90cm). Leaves dark green. Dense spikes of rose-pink flowers for about four weeks in summer. For fuller growth, pinch tips of spring growth when shoots are 6-9″ (15-23cm) long. Tolerates full sun in the North.

Zones: 4-9

Spacing: 15-18″ (38-45cm)

Propagation: division, seed

Apply a winter mulch to the less hardy perennials **before** the ground freezes. These plants generally have their crowns above the soil line.

Then, **after** the ground first freezes hard in winter, apply a mulch to protect the hardier herbaceous perennials. Use fallen leaves (preferably not from city streets), grass clippings, sawdust, coarse peat moss, or other organic material for the mulch. This protective cover must be removed as new growth starts and the ground begins to warm up next spring, or there will be delays in early growth.

Chrysanthemum coccineum

Chrysanthemum × *morifolium*

Chrysanthemum × *morifolium*

Chrysanthemum parthenium

CHRYSANTHEMUM (kri-SAN-the-mum) ○ ◑ ✂
Chrysanthemum, Daisies, Mums

Showy and reliable hardy perennials for borders, massed plantings. Long-lasting when cut. Best in fertile, well-drained soil. Leaf shape varies; often aromatic. Flowers in all colors except blue, and in many forms from daisy to full cushion. Cut top growth to ground after killing frost in fall; add winter mulch in cold climates. When new spring shoots are 6-8″ (15-20cm) long, pinch tips to encourage bushiness. Repeat pinching for later flowering varieties as needed until early summer when flower buds form.

Zones: vary by species
Spacing: 12-24″ (30-60cm)
Propagation: division

C. coccineum (kok-SIN-ee-um)
Pyrethrum, Painted Daisy

Reliable early summer daisy blossoms. Flower petals of white, red, or pink shades with yellow centers. Height 12-24″ (30-60cm); taller plants may need support. Flowers single or double, 3″ (8cm) across, borne on wiry stems above vivid green fern-like foliage. Best in cooler climates; protect from afternoon sun in southern zones. Cut stems back after flowering in summer to encourage new growth and fall flowers. Zones 3-7.

C. × *morifolium* (mo-ri-FOH-li-um)
Chrysanthemum, Garden Mum

Diverse colorful group for fall displays. Early, mid-season and late developing varieties provide color from late summer to freeze. Height 1-5′ (0.3-1.5m); taller varieties need support. Leaves usually lobed and dark green or gray-green. Zones 5-10. Many cultivars, usually grouped by flower form and plant habit:

Cushion: Double flower form; compact growth to 20″ (50cm) or less.
Daisies: Single daisy flowers with yellow centers; height varies with cultivar.
Decorative: Taller plants with double or semi-double flowers, larger than those of cushion types.
Pompon: Free-flowering varieties with small, ball-shaped blossoms; usually less than 18″ (45cm) tall.
Button: Small double flowers are less than 1″ (2.5cm) across; plants usually less than 18″ (45cm) tall.

C. parthenium (par-THEE-ni-um)
Feverfew, Matricaria

Bushy plant for summer blossom, 12-36″ (30-90cm) tall. Foliage is strongly aromatic. Button-like flowers, ¾″ (2cm) across, cover plants in mid to late summer. Zones 5-8.
Cultivars:
    'Golden Ball': yellow flowers; height to 18″ (45cm).
    'Snowball': white flowers; grows 24-36″ (60-90cm) tall.

Chrysanthemum × superbum 'Little Princess'

Chrysogonum virginianum

Cimicifuga simplex

CHRYSANTHEMUM (cont'd)

C. × *rubellum* (roo-BEL-um)
[*C. zawadskii* var. *latilobum* (zah-WARD-skee-y la-ti-LOH-bum)]
Hybrid Red Chrysanthemum
Compact and branching, masses of daisy-like flowers in late summer. Height 24-36″ (60-90cm). Leaves 4″ (10cm) long, deeply lobed. Fragrant flowers are 2-3″ (5-8cm) across, pink to rosy-red. Zones 5-9. Cultivar **'Clara Curtis'** has deep pink daisy flowers with raised yellow centers.

C. × *superbum* (soo-PERB-um)
Shasta Daisy
Free-flowering summer daisies grow 12-30″ (30-75cm) tall. Foliage deep green, coarsely toothed. Flowers white, single or double. Best in full sun and in especially well-drained locations. Zones 4-10. Single flowered cultivars:
'Alaska': hardy in zone 3; pure white petals with yellow centers; flowers 3″ (8cm) across on 24-36″ (60-90cm) stems.
'Little Princess': large flowers on compact 12″ (30cm) plant.
'Thomas Killen': vigorous and robust; extra-large flowers have double row of white petals around crested gold center; height 30″ (75cm).
Double flowered **'Aglaya'** grows to about 23″ (70cm); big flowers have fringed petals.

CHRYSOGONUM (kri-SOG-o-num) ○ ◑ ● ⚬⚬
Goldenstar, Green-and-gold
C. *virginianum* (vir-ji-nee-AH-num)
Green-and-gold
Low mat-forming plant with bright yellow blossoms from spring to early summer, longer in northern zones. Height 6-9″ (15-23cm). Best in rich, moist, well-drained soil. Good for rock garden, edging, and woodland plantings. Tolerates full sun with adequate moisture; needs at least afternoon shade in warmer climates.
Zones: 5-9
Spacing: 12-15″ (30-45cm)
Propagation: seed, division

CIMICIFUGA (si-mi-si-FEW-ga) ◑ ●
Bugbane
Tall, slender woodland plants for shaded locations with rich, moist soil. Divided foliage makes attractive, airy mound beneath blossoms. Long, slender racemes of fragrant white flowers in summer or fall.
Zones: 3-9
Spacing: 10-12″ (25-30cm)
Propagation: seed, division

C. *americana* (a-me-ri-KAH-na) **N**
American Bugbane, Rattletop, Summer Cohosh
Late summer flowers on 3-4′ (0.9-1.2m) plants.

Clematis paniculata

Clematis 'Ernest Markham'

Clematis 'Nelly Moser'

Clematis 'Jackmanii'

Clematis 'Henryi'

Clematis 'Elsa Spath'

CIMICIFUGA (cont'd)

C. racemosa (ra-se-MOH-sa) **N**
Snakeroot, Cohosh Bugbane
Late summer flowers rise on branching stems to 6-8′ (1.8-2.4m), persist for about 4 weeks. Best with constant supply of moisture.

C. simplex (SIM-pleks)
Kamchatka Bugbane
Flowers in late fall on arching stems. Height 3-4′ (0.9-1.2m).

CLEMATIS (KLEM-a-tis) ○ ◑
Clematis, Virgin's-bower
Showy, large-flowered vine for use on wall, trellis or post. Thrives where roots can be kept cool with shade, mulch, or other plants. Best in alkaline or limestone soil with constant moisture supply. Flowers 6″ (15cm) or more across, with colorful petaloid sepals and contrasting stamens. Most hybrids grow to 8-12′ (2.4-3.6m). Many need little pruning except to remove dead or unwanted growth.
Zones: 4-9
Spacing: 4′ (1.2m)
Propagation: stem cuttings
Hybrids:
　'Comtesse de Bouchard': profuse rosy lilac-pink flowers with satiny sepals, summer to early fall; vigorous — prune hard in early spring.

'Duchess of Edinburgh': double white rosette-shaped flowers in early summer and again in fall.
'Elsa Spath': large flowers in rich lavender-blue, summer to early fall.
'Ernest Markham': petunia-red flowers, late summer to fall; robust vine grows 12-16′ (3.6-4.8m); prune hard in early spring.
'Hagley Hybrid': profuse shell-pink flowers from summer to early fall; grows 6-8′ (1.8-2.4m); prune hard in early spring.
'Henryi' (HEN-ree-y): large white flowers, summer to early fall.
'Jackmanii' (jak-MAN-ee-y): profuse deep purple flowers from summer to early fall; prune hard in early spring.
'Nelly Moser': light mauve sepals have stronger pink center bands; profuse extra-large flowers in early summer and again in fall.
'Ramona': large clear blue, dark-centered flowers throughout summer. Vigorous vine grows 10-16′ (3.0-4.8m).
'The President': large dark blue to reddish-plum flowers with paler center bands and silvery reverse to sepals; resists fading; flowers continually from early summer through fall.
'Ville de Lyon': red flowers with golden centers from summer to early fall; prune hard in early spring.

C. paniculata (pa-ni-kew-LAH-ta) ⋙
Sweet Autumn Clematis
Fragrant and reliable vine or creeper with profuse white blossoms from late summer to fall. Stems grow 10-20′ (3-6m) long.

Convallaria majalis

Coreopsis rosea

Coreopsis in mixed perennial planting

CONVALLARIA   (kon-va-LAH-ri-a) ◑ ● ✕ ⋙

C. majalis   (ma-JAH-lis)
Lily-of-the-valley
Spreading, low-growing perennial with deep green foilage and delight-fully fragrant flowers in spring. Best in rich, moist soil; tolerates dry soil in shaded areas. Leaves about 8″ (20cm) long. Tiny white bell-like flow-ers hang from arching stems, 5-8 per stem, rising to about 12″ (30cm).
Zones: 2-7
Spacing: 8-12″ (20-30cm)
Propagation: division of fleshy underground stems

COREOPSIS   (ko-ree-OP-sis) ◔ ✕ **N**
Coreopsis, Tickseed
Brilliant daisy-like flowers in spring or summer, for natural and filler plantings and for cutting. Best in well-drained soil. Remove faded flowers and stems to encourage continuous blooming.
Zones: 3-10
Spacing: 10-12″ (25-30cm)
Propagation: division
Coreopsis cultivars:
   'Goldfink': single, yellow with orange centers; height to 10″ (25cm).
   'Sunray': double and semi-double golden-yellow flowers on 18-24″ (45-60cm) plants.

C. auriculata   (aw-ri-kew-LAH-ta)
Mouse Ear Coreopsis
Spring flowers golden-yellow, 1-2″ (2.5-5.0cm) across. Height 12-24″ (30-60cm). Spreads slowly. Provide consistent moisture to avoid ear-ly dormancy. Leaves dark green.
Cultivar **'Nana'** grows to 9″ (23cm), good for rock garden or edging; flowers bright orange-yellow.

C. grandiflora   (gran-di-FLOH-ra)
Coreopsis, Tickseed
Summer flowers orange to yellow, single, semi-double, or double, 1-3″ (2.5-8cm) across. Height 12-24″ (30-60cm). Upper leaves deeply lobed, lower ones simple.

C. lanceolata   (lan-see-oh-LAH-ta)
Lance Coreopsis
Summer-flowering, bushy plants to 24″ (60cm). Bright yellow flow-ers. Lance-shaped leaves on flowering stems.

C. rosea   (ROH-zee-a)
Rose Coreopsis
Late summer flowers have pink-purple petals with yellow centers. Height 12-24″ (30-60cm). Spreading coreopsis, prefers moist con-ditions.

Coronilla varia

Cortaderia selloana

Corydalis lutea

COREOPSIS (cont'd)

C. verticillata (ver-ti-si-LAH-ta)
Threadleaf Coreopsis

Summer flowering coreopsis with single, clear yellow blossoms. Height 18-36″ (45-90cm). Foliage divided, fern-like. Drought tolerant.
Cultivars:

'Grandiflora' ('Golden Showers'): bright yellow 2½″ (5cm) flowers on 18-24″ (45-60cm) plants.

'Moonbeam': prolific, soft muted-yellow flowers cover plants from early summer to fall. Height 18-24″ (45-60cm).

'Zagreb': deeper yellow flowers on compact, upright plants that grow 8-18″ (20-45cm) high.

CORONILLA (ko-roh-NIL-a) ○ ◑ ᙁ

C. varia (VAR-i-a)
Crown Vetch

Reliable and vigorous spreader, useful for erosion control on banks and as filler in large-scale plantings. Grows in any well-drained garden soil. Height 18-24″ (45-60cm). Foliage compound. Flowers in clusters, pink or pinkish-white, from early summer until frost.
Zones: 3-10
Spacing: 36″ (90cm)
Propagation: seed, division

CORTADERIA (kor-ta-DEE-ri-a) ○ ✂ ⚷

C. selloana (se-loh-AH-na)
Pampas Grass

Giant clump-forming ornamental grass, useful for accent, background, or screen. Prefers fertile, well-drained soil; must have good winter drainage. Tolerates some drought. Huge flower plumes, in silvery-white or pink, on stems up to 12′ (3.6m) tall. Cut top growth back in late winter.
Zones: 6/7-10
Spacing: 2-4′ (0.6-1.2m)
Propagation: division

CORYDALIS (ko-RID-a-lis) ◐ ●

C. lutea (LOO-tee-a)
Yellow Corydalis

Useful low, clump-forming perennial for rock garden, edging, or front of border. Height 9-15″ (23-38cm). Best where drainage is excellent. Foliage decorative, bluish-green and fern-like, may persist through mild winters. Flowers in spring, small, golden-yellow. Tolerates alkaline soils.
Zones: 5-10
Spacing: 8-10″ (20-25cm)
Propagation: seed, division in spring

Crocosmia ✕ *crocosmiiflora*

Dahlia species

CROCOSMIA (kroh-KOZ-mi-a) ○ ✄
C. ✕ *crocosmiiflora* (kroh-koz-mee-y-FLOH-ra)
Crocosmia, Montbretia

Free-flowering corm plant with brilliant colors. Useful addition to perennial plantings. Prefers moist yet well-drained soil. Height 24-36″ (60-90cm). Long, stiff leaves contrast well with other foliage in mixed plantings. Flowers in summer for about four weeks. Excellent cut flower. From zone 7 north, lift corms each fall and plant in spring. Hybrid **'Lucifer'** is vigorous form; grows to 3½′ (1.05m); bright flame-red flowers.

Zones: 5-9 (treat as annual in the North)
Spacing: plant corms 3″ (8cm) deep and 6″ (15cm) apart
Propagation: division, removal of offsets from corms

Remove dead flowers from herbaceous and bedding plants unless seed is required. Possible sites of infection are removed along with the dead and dying tissues, and at the same time the plants' energy is directed to further flower production. Spike flowers like those of *Delphinium* need not be cut right to the ground, since lateral growth on the same stem often flower later.

DAHLIA (DAHL-ya) ○ ◑ ✄

Tender perennials often planted each year for colorful massed displays or individual settings. Smaller hybrids useful in containers. Vigorous development in spring and early summer result in brilliant blooms from mid-summer to frost. Excellent cut flowers; many forms. Dahlias perform well in any good garden soil with consistent water supply. Heights range from 12″ (30cm) to 8′ (2.4m), with blossom diameters from less that 1″ (2.5cm) to 18″ (45cm). Taller plants need support. For overwintering, lift tuberous roots after first frost; treat with fungicide to minimize rotting; store in moist sand or peat moss at 40-45°F (5-10°C). Check tubers for rot and moisture need occasionally during winter months.

Zones: 8-10 (treat as annual in the North)
Spacing: 15-30″ (38-75cm)
Propagation: division of tubers before replanting in spring

Delphinium elatum Round Table Mixed

DELPHINIUM (del-FIN-i-um) ○ ✂
Delphinium, Larkspur

Colorful, elegant flower spikes rise above clumps of divided lobed foliage. Best in deep, fertile, well-drained, neutral to alkaline soil. Excellent background or accent in temperate zones. Many shades of blue, lavender, purple, and pink as well as white, yellow, and red. Taller plants need staking; flower stems tend to be hollow and brittle. Trim off fading flowers to encourage more blossom from lower side stems. When leaves yellow, cut stems back to plant base so new shoots can grow for fall flowering. Often short-lived, especially in warmer climates; easy to grow from seed.

Note: plant juices known to poison cattle.

Zones: 3-7
Spacing: 12-24″ (30-60cm)
Propagation: seed, division, stem cuttings

D. cardinale (kar-di-NAH-lee) **N**
Scarlet Larkspur

Short-lived perennial hardy in zones 8-9. Height 2-5′ (0.6-1.5m). Leaves finely divided. Scarlet flowers have long yellowish spurs.

D. elatum hybrids (e-LAH-tum)
Bee Delphinium

Summer flowering, single or double flowers in shades of blue or purple, white or pink. Height varies, 2-8′ (0.6-2.4m).

Hybrids and cultivars:

Pacific Hybrids: tall showy flower spikes; good for background, tall accent. Short-lived.

Connecticut Yankee Series: shorter, much-branched flower stems grow to 30″ (75cm). Selection **'Blue Fountains'** reliable in zone 8.

Belladonna Hybrids (*D.* × *belladonna*): compact, branching flower stems rise 3-4′ (0.9-1.2m); flowers blue or white.

'Pennant': mixed colors with wide range from rose and creamy shades to lavender and blue. Height 24-28″ (60-70cm).

Round Table Mixed: Tall, stately spires of white, pink, lavender, blue, and purple. Grows to 6′ (1.8m).

D. grandiflorum (gran-di-FLOH-rum)
Chinese Delphinium

Summer-flowering species with blue or white blossoms on 24-36″ (60-90cm) stems. Good middle or front of border accent. Blooms all summer when plants are cut back regularly.

Deschampsia caespitosa

Dianthus × allwoodii

Dianthus caryophyllus

DESCHAMPSIA (dez-KAMP-si-a) ○ ◐ ● ♣ ✿ **N**
D. caespitosa (sez-pi-TOH-sa)
Tufted Hair Grass
Dense clumps of dark green leaves form mounds 24-36″ (60-90cm) high. Flowers in summer on erect stems; large, lacy clusters (panicles) have silvery- or golden-green to purple coloring. Native of boggy soils; tolerates moist conditions.
Cultivar **'Goldschleier'** has gold-tinted flowers.
Zones: 5-10
Spacing: 18-24″ (45-60cm)
Propagation: division, seed

DIANTHUS (dee-AN-thus) ○ ✂ ♣
Pink, Carnation
Low, clump-forming perennials and biennials flower prolifically in late spring and summer. Prefer slightly alkaline soil; good drainage especially important in winter. Good in rock gardens and as edging. Narrow grass-like leaves. Flowers pink, rose, red, yellow, or white.
Zones: 2-10: see individual species
Spacing: 12-18″ (30-45cm)
Propagation: seed, division, layering, terminal stem cuttings

D. × allwoodii (awl-WOOD-ee-y)
Allwood Pink, Border Carnation
Bright, colorful hybrids bloom all summer. Flowers mostly double. Foliage gray-green. Easy. Heights range 3-20″ (8-50cm).
Cultivars:
  'Aqua': clear white double flowers; height 10-12″ (25-30cm).
  'Doris': compact plant with wonderfully fragrant flowers, salmon-pink with deep pink eye.
  'Helen': free-flowering selection in deep salmon-pink.
  'Essex Witch': miniature border carnation grows to 3-6″ (8-15cm); flower colors range from salmon to pink to white.

D. barbatus (bar-BAH-tus)
Sweet William
Self-seeding biennial has flat-topped clusters of showy blossoms in late spring of second year. Best in alkaline soil. Foliage clear green. Flower petals fringed, in red, pink, white, bicolor, often with contrasting eye colors. Excellent cut flower. Persists 2-3 years in the South; remove fading flowers to encourage fresh new growth.

Dianthus deltoides

Dianthus gratianopolitanus 'Tiny Rubies'

Dicentra spectabilis

DIANTHUS (cont'd)

D. caryophyllus (ka-ri-oh-FIL-us)
Hardy Carnation
Outdoor forms of florists' carnations have double and semi-double fragrant blossoms. Heights range 9-18″ (23-45cm) or more. Foliage gray-green. Hardy to zones 6 or 7; treat as annual in colder areas.

D. deltoides (del-TOI-deez)
Maiden Pink
Low, spreading plant forms loose mat for groundcover; useful in rock garden, on wall or ledge. Height 6-12″ (15-30cm). Foliage grass-like. Flowers red, pink, or rose. Tolerates partial shade.

D. gratianopolitanus (gra-tee-ah-noh-po-li-TAH-nus)
Cheddar Pink
Compact gray-green leafy mounds grow 9-12″ (23-30cm). Useful in rock garden, as groundcover and edging. Fragrant spring flowers in shades of rose or pink; remove faded flowers to extend season. Cultivars:
   'La Bourbille': silvery-green foliage, clear pink single flowers.
   'Spotty': red-and-white.
   'Tiny Rubies': double, deep pink flowers.

D. plumarius (ploo-MAH-ri-us)
Cottage Pink, Grass Pink
Early summer fragrant flowers rise above mounds of silver-gray leaves. Height 12-24″ (30-60cm). Good edging plant. Single or double flowers in reds, pinks, or white. Divide vigorous clumps every 2 to 3 years. Cultivars:
   'Essex Witch': white and shades of pastel pink, salmon.
   'Spring Beauty': fully double flowers in wide range of colors; spicy, clove-like fragrance.

DICENTRA (dy-SEN-tra) ◑ ✄
Elegant plants have mounding fern-like leaves and arching sprays of heart-shaped flowers from late spring to frost. Best in fertile, light soil. Good in rock gardens, borders, near woodland. Tolerates full sun in cooler climates.

Zones: 4-10
Spacing: 15-18″ (38-45cm)
Propagation: division, root cuttings, seed

Dicentra cultivars:
   'Bountiful': finely cut foliage; soft rosy-red flowers.
   'Luxuriant': blue-green foliage, cherry-red flowers; height about 15″ (45cm).
   'Zestful': large, deep rose flowers.

Dicentra cucullaria

Dicentra formosa

Dicentra eximia

Dicentra spectabilis 'Alba'

DICENTRA (cont'd)

D. cucullaria (koo-kew-LAH-ri-a) N
Dutchman's-breeches
Tuberous roots produce short-lived basal leaves and pinkish-white flowers in spring. Height 10-12″ (25-30cm). Summer dormant.

D. eximia (ek-SIM-i-a) ⋙ N
Fringed Bleeding-heart
Gray-green foliage and rose-pink flowers mound 9-18″ (23-45cm). Clumps do not spread; space 8″ (20cm) apart for groundcover.
Cultivars:
  'Alba': milky-white flowers and light green foliage.
  'Snowdrift': pure white flowers.

D. formosa (for-MOH-sa) ⋙ N
Pacific or **Western Bleeding-heart**
Deep pink, carmine, or white flowers in spring and summer. Gray-green foliage. Spreading clumps; space 8-12″ (20-30cm) for groundcover.

D. spectabilis (spek-TAH-bi-lis)
Bleeding-heart
Spring flowering species has rose-pink outer and white inner petals. Mounds 18-24″ (45-60cm). Prefers moist, well-drained soil; foliage dies out by early summer.
Cultivar **'Alba'** has light green foliage and white flowers.

DICTAMNUS (dik-TAM-nus) ◑ ✄
D. albus (AL-bus)
[*D. fraxinella* (frak-si-NEL-a)]
Fraxinella, Gas Plant, Dittany
Shrubby, reliable perennial for mid-border planting. Long lived; best left undisturbed in rich, well-drained soil. Rich green, glossy, foliage has lemon odor. Aromatic white flowers in early summer. Volatile oils can sometimes be ignited. Tolerates some shade, especially in hot climates. Best where nights are cooler. Seed pods useful in dried arrangements.
Cultivar **'Purpureus'** (pur-PEW-ree-us) has pink-purple flowers with darker veins.
Zones: 3-8
Spacing: 3-4′ (0.9-1.2m)
Propagation: seed

Dictamnus albus

Doronicum cordatum

Digitalis purpurea

DIGITALIS (di-ji-TAH-lis) ◑ ✂
Foxglove
Showy biennial or perennial. Flower spikes often one-sided, with down-ward pointing blossoms in summer. Basal foliage forms rosette. Best in partly shaded, rich, moist, well-drained soil. Good border accent or in natural planting. Self-seeding. Tolerates full sun in cooler climates.
Note: leaves are poisonous.
Zones: 4-10
Spacing: 15-18″ (38-45cm)
Propagation: seed, division (perennials)

D. grandiflora (gran-di-FLOH-ra) ♠
[*D. ambigua* (am-BIG-ew-a)]
Yellow Foxglove
Flowers creamy-yellow with brown markings inside. Height 24-36″ (60-90cm). Short-lived perennial or biennial. Self-seeding.

D. ✕ *mertonensis* (mer-ton-EN-sis)
Strawberry Foxglove
Large flowered form has rose to coppery blossoms on spikes 3-4′ (0.9-1.2m) tall. Big velvety leaves. Tetraploid hybrid; breeds true from seed. Divide plants after flowering every two years to maintain vigor.

D. purpurea (pur-PEW-ree-a)
Common or Biennial Foxglove
Purple, pink, rose, or white flowers on 4-5′ (1.2-1.5m) spikes from late spring. Wrinkled, downy foliage. Biennial form, readily self-seeds in moist semi-shade.
Hybrids and cultivars:
  'Excelsior Hybrids': big flowers held upright around stem; height 5-7′ (1.5-2.1m).
  'Foxy': branching habit, height to 30″ (75cm).
  'Giant Shirley': height to 4′ (1.2m).

DORONICUM (doh-RON-i-kum) ○◑ ✂
Leopard's-bane
D. cordatum (kor-DAH-tum)
[*D. caucasicum* (kaw-KAS-i-kum)]
Caucasian Leopard's Bane
Bright perennial for borders and early season cut flowers. Height 12-24″ (30-60cm). Prefers moist, well-drained soil. Yellow daisy-like flowers in spring. Deeply toothed leaves die back in mid-summer. Divide every 2-3 years to maintain vigor.
Zones: 4-9
Spacing: 12-18″ (30-45cm)
Propagation: division

Duchesnea indica

Echinacea purpurea 'Alba'

Echinacea purpurea

DUCHESNEA (dew-KES-nee-a) ◯◑ ᙏ
D. indica (IN-di-ka)
[*Fragaria indica* (fra-GAH-ri-a)]
Mock Strawberry
Rapidly spreading groundcover forms mat 2-3″ (5-7.5cm) thick. Grows in well-drained soil. Foliage like small strawberry leaves. Yellow flowers followed by small bitter, inedible fruits.
Zones: 2-10
Spacing: 12-18″ (30-45cm)
Propagation: division; new plantlets form on runners

ECHINACEA (e-ki-NAY-see-a) ◯ ✂ **N**
Vigorous summer-flowering perennials. Prefer well-drained soil; must have good winter drainage. Good in borders, natural plantings. Dark green leaves with whitish hairs underneath. Daisy flowers have slightly reflexed ray petals and raised central discs.
Zones: 3-10
Spacing: 18-24″ (45-60cm)
Propagation: division, root cuttings, seed

E. angustifolia (an-goos-ti-FOH-li-a)
Narrow-leaved Coneflower
Self-seeding wildflower for natural plantings. About 24″ (60cm) tall. Whitish or rose-purple flowers.

E. purpurea (pur-PEW-ree-a)
[*Rudbeckia purpurea* (rud-BEK-i-a)]
Purple Coneflower
Height 24-36″ (60-90cm). Flower have orange-brown raised centers and purple, rose, or white petals. Tolerates heat, drought, and wind. Cultivars:
  'Alba' (AL-ba): flowers creamy-white with greenish centers.
  'Bright Star': rose-colored flowers freely produced.
  'Magnus' (MAG-noos): non-reflexed, rosy ray petals.

ECHINOPS (EK-i-nops) ◯ ✂
E. ritro (RIT-roh)
Globe Thistle
Striking globular dark blue flower heads in summer. Height 2-4′ (0.6-1.2m). Prefers well-drained, dry soil; tolerates drought. Good accent for middle or back of border. Foliage whitish underneath. Useful in dried arrangements: cut before flowers are fully open.
Cultivar **'Taplow Blue'** has larger 2-3″ (5-8cm) heads of steel blue flowers.
Zones: 3-8
Spacing: 18-24″ (45-60cm)
Propagation: root cuttings, division in spring

Echinops ritro

Epimedium ✕ youngianum

Elymus arenarius

Erianthus ravennae

ELYMUS (EL-i-mus) ○ ✦
Wild Rye, Lyme Grass
E. arenarius (a-re-NAH-ri-us)
[*Leymus arenarius* (LAY-mus)]
European Dune Grass, Lyme Grass
Vigorously spreading ornamental grass prevents soil erosion especially from sandy, coastal dunes. Prefers well-drained soil. Height to 24″ (60cm). Deep gray-blue foliage color best in hot, dry climates. Tall gray-green to yellow flower clusters in late summer.
Zones: 4-10
Spacings: 18-24″ (45-60cm)
Propagation: division in early spring

EPIMEDIUM (e-pi-MEE-di-um) ◑ ● ⌇ ♠
Barrenwort
Compact, spreading groundcover with compound leaves and spring flowers. Best in shaded, humus-rich soils. Young foliage often tinged pink or red; fall color yellow, red, or bronze. Cut mature leaves back in spring so new growth and flower clusters can develop freely. Rhizomes help prevent soil erosion.
Zones: 3-8
Spacing: 8-10″ (20-25cm)
Propagation: division in late summer

E. grandiflorum (gran-di-FLOH-rum)
Longspur Barrenwort, Bishop's-hat
Mounds 8-15″ (20-38cm). Bright green foliage is beige-brown in spring, bronze in autumn. Flower color red to violet to white.

E. ✕ youngianum (yung-ee-AH-num)
Young's Barrenwort
Mounds 6-8″ (15-20cm). Sharply serrated leaflets are tinged red in spring, deep crimson in autumn. Flowers white or rose.
Cultivar **'Niveum'** (NI-vee-um) has clear white flowers.

ERIANTHUS (e-ri-AN-thus) ○ ✂ ✦
E. ravennae (ra-VEN-ee)
Ravenna Grass, Plume Grass
Strong, vigorous, and hardy giant grass that grows 10-14′ (3.0-4.2m) tall. Best in fertile, well-drained soil. Useful accent or screen. Smooth, stiff stems with 36″ (90cm) leaves that turn chestnut-brown in fall. Densely branched, silvery flower plumes open in late summer, turn beige in fall.
Zones: 5-10
Spacing: 2-5′ (0.6-1.5m)
Propagation: division, seed

Erigeron speciosus

Eryngium alpinum

ERIGERON (e-RIJ-e-ron) ○ ✂ N
Fleabane
E. speciosus (spee-si-OH-sus)
Daisy Fleabane
Reliable border perennials grow well in sandy, relatively infertile soil that drains well. Good in rock gardens or natural plantings. Height 20-30″ (50-75cm). Clusters of 1-2″ (2.5-5cm) purple daisy-like flowers rise above foliage in summer. Taller plants may need staking. Cut back after flowering to stimulate new and compact growth.
Cultivars:
  'Azure Fairy': semi-double lavender-blue flowers on 30″ (75cm) stems.
  'Foerster's Leibling': double pink flowers, height to 18″ (45cm).
Zones: 4-8
Spacing: 12″ (30cm)
Propagation: division

During dry spells, established perennials usually need less frequent, though heavier, applications of water than are required by young plants.

ERYNGIUM (e-RIN-jee-um) ○ ✂
Sea Holly
Blue-gray plants with dense flower clusters in summer. Best in well-drained sandy soil; tolerate poor, dry conditions, high salt levels. Useful accent for border, rock garden. Foliage lobed or deeply cut, spiny. Each flower head has collar of leafy bracts. Plants spread slowly, can be left undisturbed indefinitely.
Zones: 4-8
Spacing: 12-18″ (30-45cm)
Propagation: seed (species), division
E. alpinum (al-PY-num)
Alpine Sea Holly
Height 18-36″ (45-90cm). Blue conical flower heads have soft, feathery bracts. Cut off fading flowers to allow side branches to continue flowering.
E. amethystinum (a-me-THIS-ti-num)
Amethyst Sea Holly
Height 18-24″ (45-60cm). Steely-blue flowers borne in clusters on branching stems; bracts long and spiny. Hardy to zone 3.
E. giganteum (jy-GAN-tee-um)
Giant Sea Holly
Large plants grow to 4-6′ (1.2-1.8m), need wind protection. Blue flowers in big oval heads, 3-4″ (8-10cm) long, with rigid, toothed bracts. Short-lived perennial best treated as a biennial.

Erythronium americanum

Euonymus fortunei

Euonymus fortunei 'Colorata'

ERYTHRONIUM (e-rith-ROH-ni-um) ◑ N
Dog-tooth Violet, Trout Lily, Fawn Lily
Small, early spring flowering tuberous perennials for natural and wood-
land gardens. Grow in rich, moist, well-drained soil. Pendulous flow-
ers have reflexed petals. Summer dormant. Best in cooler climates
and in neutral to acid soil. Tubers must not dry out before replanting.
Zones: 4-9
Spacing: 3″ (8cm)
Propagation: seed, offsets

E. albidum (AL-bi-dum)
White Dog-tooth Violet
Mottled leaves, white or pinkish flowers. Height to 12″ (30cm).

E. americanum (a-me-ri-KAH-num)
Common Fawn Lily, Trout Lily
Mottled leaves, yellow flowers. Height to 12″ (30cm). Hardy to zone 3.

E. grandiflorum (gran-di-FLOH-rum)
Avalanche Lily
Larger species with plain green leaves and yellow flowers. Height
12-24″ (30-60cm).

EUONYMUS (ew-ON-i-mus) ○ ◑ ● ➤ ♠
E. fortunei (for-TEW-nee-y)
Wintercreeper
Spreading, clinging woody vines make dense leafy backdrop or edg-
ing in perennial plantings, rock gardens. Grows in any good garden
soil. Flowers insignificant. Susceptible to infestation by scale insects.
Cultivars:
  'Colorata' (ko-lo-RAH-ta), **Purpleleaf Wintercreeper:** rambling
    groundcover 12-15″ (30-38cm) high, will climb and cling to porous
    surfaces; foliage turns purplish-bronze in fall, holds color all
    winter.
  'Kewensis' (kew-EN-sis): small form with tiny leaves and flat, spread-
    ing stems; good for rock garden, edging; height about 3″ (8cm).
Zones: 4-10
Spacing: 12-24″ (30-60cm)
Propagation: division, cuttings

Eupatorium perfoliatum

Eupatorium purpureum

Eupatorium coelestinum

EUPATORIUM (ew-pa-TOH-ri-um) ○◑✕ N
Boneset, Thoroughwort

Vigorous perennials with showy blossoms in late summer and fall. Prefer moist, well-drained soil. Useful in borders and natural plantings. Flower heads small, in crowded clusters. Flowers best in full sun. Leaves coarse, pointed. Divide rapidly spreading clumps every 1-3 years.

Zones: 3-10
Spacing: 18-24″ (45-60cm)
Propagation: seed, division in spring

E. coelestinum (koy-les-TEE-num)
Hardy Ageratum, Mistflower, Blue Boneset

Grows 24-36″ (60-90cm). Azure-blue flat-topped flower clusters in late summer. For greater flower display, cut plants back once or twice before mid-summer.

E. perfoliatum (per-foh-li-AH-tum)
Common Boneset

White-flowered species grows naturally in moist soils. Height to 5′ (1.5m). Flowers from late summer to fall.

E. purpureum (pur-PEW-ree-um)
Joe-Pye Weed

Tall and very showy, needs abundant water supply or constantly moist soil. Height 4-7′ (1.2-2.1m). Large 8-12″ (20-30cm) leaves give off vanilla scent when crushed. Purple flowers in 12-18″ (30-45cm) clusters, in fall.

Cultivar **'Atropurpureum'** (at-roh-pur-PEW-ree-um) has purple flower stems that intensify color display.

EUPHORBIA (ew-FOR-bi-a) ○
Spurge

Spreading perennials with showy, colorful flower bracts. Best in well-drained soil. Plants can remain undisturbed indefinitely.

Note: milky sap can cause irritation; do not allow it to contact open cuts or sores.
Zones: 3-9
Spacing: 18-24″ (45-60cm)
Propagation: seed

E. epithymoides (e-pi-ti-MI-deez)
[*E. polychroma* (po-li-KROH-ma)]
Cushion Spurge

Spreading clumps grow 12-18″ (30-45cm) tall. Yellow flower bracts open in early spring. Foliage pale green, turning reddish in fall. Shade from afternoon sun in hot climates. Tolerates dry soil.

Euphorbia epithymoides

Euphorbia myrsinites

Euphorbia griffithii 'Fireglow'

Festuca ovina var. *glauca*

EUPHORBIA (cont'd)

E. griffithii (gri-FITH-ee-y)
Griffith's Spurge
Numerous orange-red flower bracts in summer. Upright habit, 24-36″ (60-90cm) tall. Leaves medium green with pale pink midribs. Needs constant moisture.
Cultivar **'Fireglow'** has more intense coloring, with orange-brown stems.

E. myrsinites (mer-si-NEE-teez) ⚬♠
Myrtle Euphorbia
Trailing stems clothed with gray-green foliage. Best in dry, well-drained soil. Useful in rock plantings. Yellow flower bracts in spring rise 6-9″ (15-23cm). Tolerates heat well.

FESTUCA (fes-TOO-ka) ○◑♠ ⚼
Fescue
Ornamental forms of turf grass grow in tufts with flat or rolled leaf-blades. Best in light, well-drained soil without added nutrients. Useful in edgings, rock gardens. Tolerates some shade though blue-green forms develop best color in full sun.
Zones: 4-10
Spacing: 15-18″ (38-45cm)
Propagation: division

F. cinerea cultivars:
 'Klose': foliage dark green; mounds to 8″ (20cm).
 'Solling': foliage powder-blue; mounds to 6″ (15cm).

F. muelleri (MEW-le-ry)
Foliage soft blue-green. Mounds to 8″ (20cm).

F. ovina (oh-VY-na)
Sheep's Fescue
Slender, rolled, very fine and soft thread-like leaves grow about 6″ (15cm) long. Height 8-12″ (20-30cm). Tufts do not spread. Flowers in one-sided panicles.

F. ovina var. glauca (glaw-ka), **Blue Fescue,** has silvery-blue, arching foliage. Its cultivar **'Sea Urchin'** is more rigid and compact, growing to height of 10″ (25cm).

F. tenuifolia (ten-ew-i-FOH-li-a)
Hair Fescue
Fine, velvety, yellow-green foliage on mounds 8″ (20cm) high. Spring and early summer flowers followed by deep reddish-bronze seedheads.

Filipendula palmata

Filipendula rubra

Filipendula vulgaris

FILIPENDULA (fi-li-PEN-dew-la) ○ ◐
Meadowsweet

Dainty summer-flowering perennials for moist locations. Best in neutral to alkaline soils. Useful in semi-shaded borders, natural plantings. Attractive lobed or divided leaves. Flowers white or pink, in foamy, loose clusters. Can remain undisturbed indefinitely.

Zones: 4-8
Spacing: 24-36″ (60-90cm)
Propagation: seed (species), division

F. palmata (pal-MAH-ta)
Siberian Meadowsweet

Multitudes of 6″ (15cm) flower clusters rise above leaves. Pink color turns white as flowers mature. Height 3-4′ (0.9-1.2m). Prefers very moist soil, especially in full sun.

F. rubra (ROO-bra) **N**
Queen-of-the-prairie

Tall yet wind tolerant plant has pink to peach flowers in 6-9″ (15-23cm) open clusters. Grows rapidly in boggy conditions. Height 6-8′ (1.8-2.4m).
Cultivar **'Venusta'** (ve-NUS-ta) has deeper pink flowers.

F. vulgaris (vul-GAH-ris)
[*F. hexapetala* (hek-sa-PET-a-la)]

Creamy-white flowers, often tinged pink, in flattish clusters. Leaves fern-like. Height 24-36″ (60-90cm). Prefers constant moisture but, having tuberous roots, tolerates drier soils than other species.
Cultivar **'Flore-pleno'** (FLOH-re-PLEE-noh) has double flowers, grows to 24″ (60cm).

○ = Full Sun	♠ = Evergreen
◐ = Partial Shade	**N** = Native or Naturalized Plant
● = Shade	⚥ = Ornamental Grass
⌇ = Groundcover	✂ = Cut Flowers

Gaillardia × *grandiflora* 'Baby Cole'

Galeobdolon luteum

GAILLARDIA (gay-LAR-di-a) ○ ✂ **N**
G.* × *grandiflora (gran-di-FLOH-ra)
Blanketflower
Vigorous plants for average to poor, well-drained or dry soils. Useful in borders and natural plantings in full sun. Leafy, erect, branching plants grow 24-36″ (60-90cm) tall. Taller varieties may need staking. Colorful 2-4″ (5-10cm) daisies in red, gold, and maroon from summer to frost. Remove faded flowers for continued display. Divide clumps every 2-3 years to prevent overcrowding. Shortlived in moist, fertile soils; intolerant of heavy wet winter conditions. Tolerates heat and drought. Naturalized hybrid of two native species.
Cultivars:
'Baby Cole': dwarf form has red, banded yellow flowers; height 6-8″ (15-20cm).
'Burgundy': rich wine-red flowers; height 24-36″ (60-90cm).
'Dazzler': golden-tipped petals have maroon centers; height to 24″ (60cm).
'Goblin': dwarf form with yellow-tipped red flowers; height 9-12″ (23-30cm).

Zones: 2-10
Spacing: 10-12″ (25-30cm)
Propagation: seed, division

GALEOBDOLON (ga-lee-OB-do-lon) ○ ◑ ● ⤳
G. luteum (LOO-tee-um)
[*Lamiastrum galeobdolon* (la-mi-AS-trum)]
Golden Deadnettle, Yellow Archangel
Spreading stoloniferous perennial grows 12-24″ (30-60cm) high. Thrives in any well-drained soil. Useful as groundcover, container plant, or for naturalizing. Dense clusters of yellow flowers in spring. May become invasive.
Cultivars:
'Herman's Pride': striking silvery markings on foliage; habit less aggressive.
'Variegatum' (ve-ri-e-GAH-tum): silver-variegated foliage.

Zones: 3-10
Spacing: 15-18″ (38-45cm)
Propagation: division

Movable containers with accent plants enable you to rearrange the garden with neither the labor of digging and replanting, nor the wait while soil-grown accents become established.

Galium odoratum

Gaura lindheimeri

Gentiana acaulis

GALIUM (GAL-i-um) ○ ◑ ➥
Bedstraw, Cleavers
G. odoratum (oh-do-RAH-tum)
[*Asperula odorata* (as-PER-ew-la oh-do-RAH-ta)]
Sweet Woodruff
Spreading perennial grows 9-12″ (23-30cm) high. Good groundcover around shrubs, in borders, wooded areas. Best in moist, well-drained soils; partial shade in warmer zones. Glossy green foliage. White, starry flowers in loose clusters from spring to early summer. Stems, leaves, and flowers sweetly scented.
Zones: 4-9
Spacing: 12″ (30cm)
Propagation: division

GAURA (GAW-ra) ○ ◑ **N**
G. lindheimeri (lind-HY-me-ry)
White Gaura
Clusters of 1″ (2.5cm) white to rose flowers rise 3-4′ (0.9-1.2m) over foliage in late spring and summer. Best in rich, well-drained soil. Useful for border, natural planting. Remove fading flowers to extend display into fall. Tolerates heat and humidity.
Zones: 5-10
Spacing: 18-24″ (45-60cm)
Propagation: seed, division

GENTIANA (jen-shi-AH-na) ○ ◑ ●
Compact plants with open trumpet-shaped flowers in shades of blue. Need moist, humus-rich acid soil with pH 5.0-6.5. Grow in rock garden with liberal moisture and shade in warmer areas, and in sheltered borders and woodland plantings. Leaves form thick mat beneath flowers. Established plants best left undisturbed.
Zones: 4-8
Spacing: 12-18″ (30-45cm)
Propagation: seed, sown when ripe in fall

G. acaulis (a-KAW-lis)
Stemless Gentian
Alpine species best in cool, moist locations. Large sky-blue flowers in spring. Height to 4″ (10cm).

G. septemfida (sep-TEM-fi-da)
Crested Gentian
Upright, arching stems mound 8-12″ (20-30cm) high. Summer flowers dark blue. Tolerates well-drained clay soils.

Geranium 'Claridge Druce'

Geranium sanguineum var. striatum

Geranium dalmaticum

Geranium himalayense

GERANIUM (je-RAY-ni-um) ○ ◑
Cranesbill, Geranium

Spreading, branching perennials with flowers in shades of mauve, blue, pink, red, and white. Good in almost any moist, well-drained soil. Distinctive lobed or dissected leaves that often change color in fall. Plants thrive when divided every 2-4 years. Characteristic fruits shaped like crane's beak or bill.

Zones: 4-8: see individual species
Spacing: 12-15″ (30-38cm)
Propagation: division, cuttings (stem and root)

Geranium cultivar:
   'Claridge Druce': produces 2″ (5cm) lilac-pink flowers all summer, grows 18″ (45cm) high.

G. cinereum (si-NE-ree-um)
Grayleaf Cranesbill

Semi-evergreen, 6-12″ (15-30cm) mounding plant with red or pink flowers in spring. Useful at front of border, in rock garden. Best in zones 5-7.

G. dalmaticum (dal-MAT-i-kum)
Dalmatian Cranesbill

Low-growing, spreading semi-evergreen for rock garden, edging. Height 4-6″ (10-15cm); taller when grown in shade. Leaves red-orange in fall. Late spring flowers mauve or light pink.

G. endressii (en-DRES-ee-y)
Endress's Geranium, Pyrenean Cranesbill

Summer flowers light pink. Height 15-18″ (38-45cm). Useful in rock garden, border. Glossy semi-evergreen foliage. Good drainage essential. Cultivar **'Wargrave Pink'** has distinctive salmon-pink flowers.

G. himalayense (hi-mah-lay-EN-see)
[*G. grandiflorum* (gran-di-FLOH-rum)]
Lilac Cranesbill, Lilac Geranium

Spreading clumps with 1½-2″ (4-5cm) violet-blue summer flowers. Height 10-15″ (25-38cm). Useful for informal edging, border. Leaves bright red in fall. Best in full sun with consistent moisture.

G. macrorrhizum (mak-roh-REE-zum) ⋙
Bigroot Geranium

Semi-evergreen, spreading, rhizomatous plant forms dense leafy carpet. Height 15-18″ (38-45cm). Foliage changes color in fall. Spring to summer flowers purplish-magenta. Tolerates heat.
Cultivar **'Album'** (AL-bum) has white petals and pink sepals.

G. maculatum (ma-kew-LAH-tum) **N**
Spotted Geranium, Wild Cranesbill

Self-seeding wildflower clumps grow 18-30″ (45-75cm) high. Grows well in sunny, moist locations. Good for border, natural garden. Late spring flowers pinkish-lilac, in clusters. Zones 5-8.

Geum quellyon

GERANIUM (cont'd)

G. robertianum (roh-bur-tee-AH-num) **N**
Herb Robert, Red Robin
Sprawling wild geranium 12-18″ (30-45cm). Clusters of tiny reddish flowers all summer. Best in well-drained, partly shaded natural plantings.

G. sanguineum (san-GWIN-ee-um) ⚘
Blood-red Cranesbill
Free-flowering, mounding plant grows 9-12″ (23-30cm). Useful edging, front of borders, natural plantings. Magenta flowers in spring. Fall foliage crimson-red. Tolerates heat. Hardy to zone 3.

G. s. var. striatum (stry-AH-tum)
[*G. s. var. lancastriense*, 'Lancastriense' (lan-kas-tree-EN-see)]
Short, spreading form grows 4-6″ (10-15cm) high. Light pink flowers have darker veins.

GEUM (JEE-um) ○◑✂
Avens
Colorful spring to summer flowers with dark green compound leaves. Best with ample moisture, good drainage, and protection from hot afternoon sun. Red, orange, or yellow, single or double flowers. Remove faded flowers to extend season.
Zones: 5-10
Spacing: 10-12″ (20-30cm)
Propagation: division, seed

G. × borisii (bo-RIS-ee-y)
Boris Avens
Orange-scarlet single for front of borders, edging, or rock garden. Height 9-12″ (23-30cm). Rounded, lobed foliage. Main flowering late spring to early summer, then intermittently to fall. Prefers partial shade.

G. macrophyllum (mak-roh-FIL-um) **N**
Large-leaved Geum
Spreading, rhizomatous wildflower with ¼″ (6mm) yellow flowers and big leaves. Height 12-36″ (30-90cm). Prefers sandy, acid to neutral soil (pH 6.0-7.0). Space at least 12″ (30cm) apart.

G. quellyon (KEL-yon)
Chilean Avens
Single to double spring flowers on 20-24″ (50-60cm) plants. Short-lived border perennials; divide every 2-3 years to maintain vigor. Cultivars:
  'Lady Stratheden': semi-double, buttercup yellow flowers.
  'Mrs. Bradshaw': semi-double scarlet flowers.

G. triflorum (tri-FLOH-rum) **N**
Prairie Smoke
Rapidly spreading wildflower with distinctive plumed fruit. Prefers sandy, acid to neutral soil (pH 6.0-7.0). Unusual, drooping, cream to pink flowers. Space at least 12″ (30cm) apart.

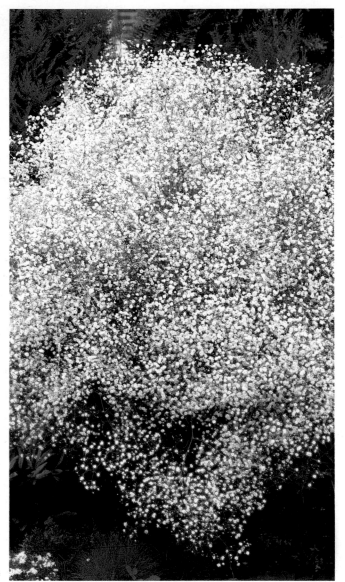

Glyceria maxima 'Variegata'

Gypsophila paniculata

GLYCERIA (gli-SEE-ri-a) ○ ✔
G. maxima 'Variegata' (MAK-si-ma ve-ri-e-GAH-ta)
[*G. aquatica* 'Variegata' (ak-WAT-i-ka ve-ri-e-GAH-ta)]
Manna Grass, Sweet Grass
Spreading ornamental grass has smoothly arching leaves, brilliantly striped in green and white or creamy-yellow. Height to 36″ (90cm). Best in moist, fertile soil. Border or moderate size accent. Early spring foliage has pinkish color. Leaf-blades 2″ (5cm) wide and 20″ (50cm) long, arching from erect stems. Flowers in branching clusters (panicles).
Zones: 5-10
Spacing: 12-15″ (30-38cm)
Propagation: division in spring

GYPSOPHILA (jip-SOF-i-la) ○ ✂
Baby's-breath
Airy, graceful perennials produce profusion of tiny white or pink flowers in summer. Prefers deep, well-drained, alkaline soil (pH 7.5 or higher). Best when established clumps are left undisturbed.
Zones: 4-8
Spacing: 24-36″ (60-90cm)
Propagation: seed, division, cuttings

G. paniculata (pa-ni-kew-LAH-ta)
Baby's-breath
Cloud-like masses of white blossoms in mid-summer. Height 24-36″ (60-90cm). Narrow, gray-green foliage. Cut back after first flowering to encourage fall production. Excellent for cut flowers, fresh or dried.
Cultivars:
  'Bristol Fairy': double white flowers.
  'Perfecta': robust form has larger double white flowers.
  'Pink Fairy': smaller variety with double pink flowers; height to 18″ (45cm).

G. repens (REE-penz) ⋙
Creeping Baby's-breath
Low-growing species for rock garden, edging, front of border. Forms mat 4-8″ (10-20cm) deep. Gray foliage. White to lilac flowers.

> After digging the flower bed to loosen the ground and to mix in added fertilizer and soil amendments, rake the surface so the soil is uniform and level before planting.

Hakonechloa macra

Hedera helix

Helianthemum nummularium

HAKONECHLOA (ha-koh-nee-KLOH-a) ○ ⚭

H. macra (MAY-kra)
Rhizomatous ornamental grass; height to 18″ (45cm). Best in fertile, well-drained soil. Useful in borders, as accent. Soft, gracefully arching, yellow-green leaves. Flowers in late summer with delicate, open panicles. Intolerant of full sun. Spreads slowly.
Cultivar **'Aureola'** (aw-ree-OH-la) has bright yellow leaves with fine green stripes, attractive buff color in fall.
Zones: 5-10
Spacing: 12-15″ (30-38cm)
Propagation: division

Water herbaceous perennials during dry spells. Give sufficient water to penetrate the ground to some depth, for a mere sprinkling will encourage the growth of surface roots that succumb rapidly to continued drought. A summer mulch helps retain soil moisture.

HEDERA (HED-e-ra) ◐ ● ✂ ⚭ ♠
Ivy
Trailing woody vines that cling to porous surfaces. Grow in any good garden soil. Useful for containers, groundcover, and cut foliage. Leaves variable. Insignificant yellowish flower clusters in fall. Dry, warm conditions encourage spider mite infestations.
Zones: 5-10
Spacing: 12″ (30cm)
Propagation: cuttings

H. canariensis (ka-ne-ree-EN-sis)
Algerian or **Canary Ivy**
Robust vine quickly fills area. Wine-red stems, bright green foliage turns bronze-green in winter. Big leaves as wide as 5-7″ (13-18cm). Hardy only to zone 7. Variegated cultivars.

H. helix (HEE-liks)
English Ivy
Fine-leaved ivy with dark green foliage up to 4″ (10cm) across. Many size, form, and color variations.

Helenium autumnale

HELENIUM (he-LEE-ni-um) ○ ✂ **N**
Sneezeweed
Adaptable, daisy-flowered perennial with showy orange to yellow blossoms in late summer and fall. Useful in natural planting; stake for support in borders. Tolerates cold climates, moist soils.
Zones: 3-10
Spacing: 12-18″ (30-45cm)
Propagation: division, seed

H. autumnale (aw-tum-NAH-lee)
Common Sneezeweed, Helen's Flower
Plants grow 3-5′ (0.9-1.5m). Sprays of yellow or mahogany daisies borne on dark brown-black stems. Leaves 4-6″ (10-15cm) long. Several named cultivars.

H. bigelovii (bi-ge-LOH-vee-y)
Bigelow Sneezeweed
Yellow flowers have brownish-yellow central discs. Height about 4′ (1.2m).

HELIANTHEMUM (hee-li-AN-the-mum) ○ ⌁ ♠
Sun Rose, Rock Rose
H. nummularium (nu-mew-LAH-ri-um)
Common Sun Rose
Low, spreading shrubby perennial with woody stems and summer flowers. Height 12-24″ (30-60cm). Best in poor, rocky or sandy, well-drained alkaline soil. Good for rock garden, dry rocky bank, edging. Dark green to gray foliage. Trim after first bloom to encourage later flowering. Cultivars have yellow, orange, red, pink, or white, single or double flowers. Need protection from severe winter temperatures.
Zones: 5-8
Spacing: 18″ (45cm)
Propagation: seed, cuttings

A warm, protected planting site often extends the northern limit of a plant's hardiness zones. Sheltered, cool, and somewhat moist locations may extend the same limit further south.

Helianthus decapetalus

Helleborus orientalis

Helleborus niger

Helictotrichon sempervirens

Heliopsis helianthoides

Herniaria glabra

HELIANTHUS (hee-li-AN-thus) ○ ✕ **N**
H. decapetalus (de-ka-PET-a-lus)
[*H.* ✕ *multiflorus* (mul-ti-FLOH-rus)]
Thin-leaved Sunflower
Vigorous, upright perennial. Height 3-5′ (0.9-1.5m). Grows in any moist, well-drained soil. Big, oval, coarsely toothed leaves. Late summer daisy flowers yellow or yellow-orange, as big as 5″ (13cm) across. Stake to support tall plants.
Cultivar **'Flore-pleno'** (FLOH-re-PLEE-noh) has fully double, bright yellow flowers.
Zones: 3-10
Spacing: 18-24″ (45-60cm)
Propagation: seed, division

HELICTOTRICHON (he-lik-toh-TRY-kon) ○ ♠ ⚘
Avena, Oat Grass
H. sempervirens (sem-per-VY-renz)
Blue Oat Grass, Avena
Ornamental grass with showy, blue-brown flower panicles that rise high over arching blue-gray foliage in summer. Best in well-drained neutral to alkaline soil. Height 20-36″ (50-90cm). Tolerates drought once established, and some shade.
Zones: 4-10
Spacing: 12-15″ (30-38cm)
Propagation: division, seed

HELIOPSIS (hee-li-OP-sis) ○ ✕ **N**
Oxeye
H. helianthoides (hee-li-an-THOI-deez)
Sunflower Heliopsis
Showy, informal perennial for border or natural planting. Grows 3-6′ (0.9-1.8m). Best in well-drained soil. Serrated leaves 4-5″ (10-13cm) long. Yellow sunflower-like blossoms in summer, 2-3″ (5-8cm) across.
H. helianthoides subsp. **scabra** (SKAY-bra), **Rough Heliopsis,** has rough, hairy foliage and fewer, orange-yellow flowers.
Cultivar **'Incomparabilis'** (in-kom-pa-RAB-i-lis) has 3″ (8cm) warm orange single to semi-double flowers with overlapping petals.
Zones: 3-9
Spacing: 24″ (60cm)
Propagation: seed, division

In 1890, the first recorded hybridization of daylilies *(Hemerocallis)* was carried out by English schoolteacher George Yeld. After two years, he introduced the first cultivar, 'Apricot'.

Hemerocallis 'Stella de Oro'

Hemerocallis 'Heart's Afire'

Hemerocallis 'Beloved Country'

Hemerocallis 'Golden Gate'

HELLEBORUS (he-LEB-oh-rus) ○ ◑ ✄ ♠

Low-growing, perennials that bloom from winter to early spring. Prefer moist, neutral to slightly alkaline soils (pH 7.0-8.0). Dark green, divided, nearly stemless foliage. Clusters of greenish, white, pink, or purple flowers on fleshy stems. Heavy fibrous roots are brittle, so handle with care. Established clumps can remain undisturbed indefinitely. Protect from damage by ice and snow.

Note: all plant parts poisonous.
Zones: 4-8
Spacing: 12-15″ (30-38cm)
Propagation: seed, division

H. niger (NY-jer)
Christmas Rose
Blooms from late fall to early spring, depending on climate. Height 12-18″ (30-45cm). Cup-shaped flowers have prominent yellow stamens, are borne on red-spotted stems.

H. orientalis (o-ree-en-TAH-lis)
Lenten Rose
Winter to early spring flowers are white, pink, or purple, sometimes with darker spots. Height 15-18″ (38-45cm). Leafy flower bracts.

HEMEROCALLIS (he-me-roh-KAL-is) ○ ◑ N
Daylily
Adaptable, low maintenance lily-like garden plants have become naturalized in many areas. Numerous cultivars in wide range of color. Heights vary from miniatures of 15-18″ (38-45cm) to giants of 4′ (1.2m) or taller. Best in fertile, moist, well-drained soil. Tolerate heat and drought. Good in borders, massed for accent, and in natural plantings. Long leaves form big clumps. Flowers single or double, sizes vary from 3-8″ (8-20cm) and more.
Zones: 3-10
Spacing: 18-24″ (45-60cm)
Propagation: division, seed (species)

HERNIARIA (he-ni-AH-ri-a) ○ ⌇
H. glabra (GLAB-ra)
Herniary, Rupturewort
Low, moss-like creeper for rock garden, edging, between paving stones. Height 2-4″ (5-10cm). Summer flowers greenish-white.
Zones: 5-9
Spacing: 10-12″ (25-30cm)
Propagation: seed, division

Hesperis matronalis

Heuchera sanguinea

Heuchera sanguinea

HESPERIS (HES-pe-ris) ○ ◐ N
H. matronalis (ma-troh-NAH-lis)
Dame's-rocket, Sweet Rocket
Upright, branching self-seeded biennial, naturalized in eastern states. Height 24-36″ (60-90cm). Needs consistent moisture in well-drained soil. Plant in natural garden, informal border. Leaves sharply pointed. Flowers from late spring in second year from seed: long fragrant clusters of white, mauve, or purple.
Zones: 4-8
Spacing: 15-18″ (38-45cm)
Propagation: seed

HEUCHERA (HEW-ke-ra) ○ ◐ ✂ ♠ N
Alumroot
Low non-spreading mounds of distinctive foliage topped by airy clusters of small, bell-like flowers in late spring and summer. Prefers rich, well-drained soil; must have good winter drainage. Mulch in winter where freezing and thawing ground can cause heaving. Tolerates stony locations.
Zones: 4-10
Spacing: 12″ (30cm)
Propagation: division, seed

Heuchera cultivars:
  'Palace Purple': ivy-leaved, deep mahogany-red foliage fades to bronze-green in heat; flowers white, to height of 12-24″ (30-60cm).
  'Green Ivory': profuse greenish-white flower clusters rise 30-36″ (75-90cm).

H. micrantha (my-KRAN-tha)
Small-flowered Alumroot
Foliage gray-green and heart-shaped. Flowers yellowish-white, rise 12-24″ (30-60cm).

H. sanguinea (san-GWIN-ee-a)
Coralbells
Mounds of heart-shaped or roundish, lobed foliage with bronze to green coloring. Flowers white to red, rising 12-24″ (30-60cm). Remove faded flower stems to extend long season.

Local nurseries and responsible mail order companies generally make valid recommendations of plants for a given area. Other sources of advice are gardeners in the area and your local Agricultural Extension Agent.

Hosta undulata 'Variegata'

Hosta sieboldiana 'Elegans'

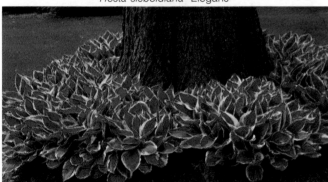

Hosta undulata 'Albo-marginata'

Hosta 'Royal standard'

HOSTA (HOS-ta) ○ ◑ ● ⋈
Hosta, Plantain Lily

Reliable leafy perennials with variously marked and colored foliage. Best in moist, rich, well-drained soil. Useful for edging, low hedge, groundcover, border accent, for planting in containers, among shrubs and trees. Summer flower clusters are white to purple, opening close to foliage or rising to 3-5′ (0.9-1.5m). Slow-growing clumps rarely need dividing. Blue and variegated foliage best in part or full shade. Heights range from 6″ (15cm) to 36″ (90cm); clumps can spread to twice their height. Use bait to deter slugs and snails.

Zones: 3-9
Spacing: 12-24″ (30-60cm)
Propagation: division

Hosta cultivars:

  'Francee': heart-shaped leaves in rich green with contrasting white edges; colors hold well in full sun. Height 12-24″ (30-60cm). Flowers lavender.

  'Frances Williams': heavily textured blue-green leaves have broad golden-yellow edges. Height 12-24″ (30-60cm). Flowers white.

  'Golden Tiara': quickly forms compact mounds 6-12″ (15-30cm) high. Heart-shaped leaves have wide golden margins. Flowers deep lavender.

  'Krossa Regal': large frosty-blue foliage more upright than spreading. Height 24-36″ (60-90cm). Flowers lavender, rise to 5′ (1.5m).

  'Royal Standard': glossy green, spreading oval leaves. Height 18-24″ (45-60cm). Pure white, fragrant flowers.

H. fortunei 'Aureo-marginata'
(for-TEW-nee-y aw-ree-oh-mar-ji-NAH-ta)
Dark green leaves have bright golden-yellow borders. Height 12-24″ (30-60cm). Flowers lilac.

H. sieboldiana 'Elegans' (see-bohl-di-AH-na EL-e-ganz)
Big, heavily textured blue-gray rounded leaves become distinctly corrugated with maturity. Height 24-36″ (60-90cm). White flowers in compact clusters.

H. undulata 'Albo-marginata' (un-dew-LAH-ta al-bo-mar-ji-NAH-ta)
Large green leaves have broad white edges. Height 12-24″ (30-60cm). Flowers white.

H. undulata 'Variegata' (ve-ri-e-GAH-ta)
[*H. u.* 'Medio-picta' (mee-di-oh-PIK-ta)]
Undulating leaves have white centers and green margins. Height 12-24″ (30-60cm). Flowers lilac.

Houttuynia cordata 'Chameleon'

Iberis sempervirens

Hypericum calycinum

Imperata cylindrica 'Rubra'

HOUTTUYNIA (hoo-TY-ni-a) ◗ ● ⌇
H. cordata (kor-DAH-ta)
Chameleon Plant
Vigorous, spreading, rhizomatous perennial for moist soils or shallow water. Useful groundcover in boggy places. Leaves heart-shaped, green. Flowers white with prominent centers. Variegated cultivar **'Chameleon'** ('Cameleon') has irregular markings in yellow, bronze, pink, and scarlet-red on 3″ (8cm) leaves. Height 6-9″ (15-23cm).
Zones: 3-8
Spacing: 12-15″ (30-38cm)
Propagation: division

HYPERICUM (hy-PER-i-kum) ○ ⌇
H. calycinum (ka-li-SEE-num)
St.-John's-wort
Spreading woody perennial has bright yellow cup-shaped summer flowers. Height 15-18″ (38-45cm). Prefers well-drained soil. Useful for edging, rock garden, or sunny banks where soil will be held in place by prostrate, rooting branches. Foliage blue-green, purplish in fall, evergreen in warmer areas. Shear vigorous plants every few years.
Zones: 5-10
Spacing: 15-24″ (38-60cm)
Propagation: seed, division, cuttings

IBERIS (y-BEE-ris) ○ ⌇ ▲
Candytuft
I. sempervirens (sem-per-VY-renz)
Evergreen Candytuft
Spreading woody perennial mounds to 9-12″ (23-30cm). Best in moist, well-drained soil. Useful edging, rock garden, border plant. Narrow leaves about 1½″ (4cm) long. Clusters of white flowers from late spring to early summer. Shear lightly after flowering to encourage new leafy growth. Cut woody stems back every 1-2 years.
Zones: 3-10
Spacing: 12-15″ (30-38cm)
Propagation: seed, division, cuttings

IMPERATA (im-PER-ay-ta) ○◗ ● ⌇
I. cylindrica **'Rubra'** (si-LIN-dri-ka ROO-bra)
Japanese Blood Grass
Ornamental grass with tufts of striking deep red leaf blades. Best in fertile, moist, yet well-drained soil. Good in borders, rock gardens. Upright, open habit, height 12-24″ (30-60cm). Rhizomatous; spreads slowly. Cultivar **'Red Baron'** has intense color that remains throughout growing season.
Zones: 5-10
Spacing: 15-18″ (38-45cm)
Propagation: division

Incarvillea delavayi

Iris cristata

Inula ensifolia

Iris germanica

INCARVILLEA (in-kar-VIL-ee-a) ○ ◑
I. delavayi (de-la-VAY-y)
Hardy Gloxinia
Warm climate perennial with big trumpet-shaped pink flowers in early summer. Clumps mound 18-24″ (45-60cm) high. Best left undisturbed in humus-rich sandy, well-drained soil. Useful in rock gardens, protected borders; select position sheltered from winter winds. Foliage deeply divided. Flowers borne in clusters. Remove faded blossoms to extend season.
Zones: 6-10
Spacing: 12-15″ (30-38cm)
Propagation: seed, division

INULA (IN-ew-la) ○ ✄
I. ensifolia (en-si-FOH-li-a)
Swordleaf Inula
Low, vigorous perennial with brilliant golden-yellow daisy flowers in late summer. Height 12-24″ (30-60cm). Grows in any moist, well-drained soil. Good in rock garden, at front of border. Small, lance-shaped leaves. Flowers borne singly on wiry stems. Tolerates moist soils. Divide exuberant clumps every 2-3 years.
Zones: 3-9
Spacing: 12-18″ (30-45cm)
Propagation: seed, division

IRIS (Y-ris) ○ ✄
Flag, Fleur-de-lis
Spreading rhizomatous plants with sword-like leaves and distinctive, showy, colorful flowers from late spring to summer. Most prefer moist well-drained soil and tolerate periods of drought; some need constant moisture. Distinctive flowers: three petals called falls are reflexed, and three called standards turn upwards.
Zones: 3-10: see individual species
Spacing: 10-18″ (20-45cm)
Propagation: division

I. cristata (kris-TAH-ta) **N**
(Crested Iris)
Height 3-6″ (8-15cm). Flowers pale lilac. Plant rhizomes at surface of well-drained soil. Good for rock garden, front of border. Zones 3-8.

I. germanica (jer-MAN-i-ka)
Bearded Iris, German Iris
Many colorful selections provide displays from late spring. Yellow, orange, white, lilac, purple, and bicolor flowers. Plant rhizomes at surface of well-drained soil. Height varies 8-36″ (20-90cm). Useful accent in border or in front of wall or shrubs.

Iris kaempferi

Kniphofia uvaria

Iris sibirica

Kniphofia uvaria

IRIS (cont'd)

I. kaempferi (KEM-fe-ry)
[*I. ensata* (en-SAH-ta)]
Japanese Iris

Summer-flowering irises that grow 24-36″ (60-90cm) tall. Prefer slightly acid soil, moist or boggy conditions, partial shade. Useful at edge of woodland, near pond. Flower up to 10″ (25cm) across, with shorter, flatter standard petals. Many selections with single, double, or peony-style flowers: colors from white to pink to purple to blue. Zones 5-9.

I. pumila (PEW-mi-la)
Dwarf Bearded Iris

Short, 4-8″ (10-20cm) iris with spring flowers in many colors, borne one per stem. Use in rock garden, at front of border. Leaves grow longer after flowering. Plant rhizomes at surface of well-drained soil. Zones 4-8.

I. sibirica (si-BI-ri-ka)
Siberian Iris

Summer flowers in shades of blue or white. Height 24-36″ (60-90cm). Prefer slightly acid soil, moist or boggy conditions, partial shade. Useful at edge of woodland, near pond. Tolerate drier conditions when watered throughout growing season. Divide clumps only after flower production falls off.

I. versicolor (ver-SIK-o-lor) **N**
Wild Iris, Wild Flag

Selfseeding wildflower of wet soils. Prefer slightly acid soil, moist or boggy conditions, partial shade. Useful at edge of woodland, near pond.
Note: rhizome juices may cause dermatitis.

KNIPHOFIA (ny-FOH-fi-a) ○ ✄ ♠
Torch Lily, Poker Plant, Tritoma
K. uvaria (oo-VAH-ri-a)
Red-hot-poker, Common Torch Lily

Poker-like flower clusters rise in summer from clumps of long, narrow gray-green leaves. Height 2-4′ (0.6-1.2m). Grow in well-drained garden soil. Flower color red, orange-red, yellow, coral, or cream. Plant no deeper than 2-3″ (5-8cm). For winter, remove flower stems; tie leaves together to protect crown; mulch with dry material to keep moisture out, to prevent freezing or heaving. Or lift crowns each fall and store through winter in cool moist sand. Divide older clumps.
Zones: 5-10
Spacing: 18-24″ (45-60cm)
Propagation: seed, division, offsets

LAMIASTRUM GALEOBDOLON
see *Galeobdolon luteum* on page 65.

Lamium maculatum 'Beacon Silver'

Lathyrus latifolius

Lavandula species

LAMIUM (LAY-mium) ◯◐●₩
L. maculatum (ma-kew-LAH-tum)
Spotted Deadnettle
Spreading perennial forms leafy mat 8-12″ (20-30cm) high. Thrives in any well-drained soil. Good groundcover, especially for shaded areas. Variegated foliage. Clusters of pink to purple or white flowers in spring. Grows vigorously; may become invasive.
Subspecies **aureum** (AW-ree-um) has golden-yellow leaves with creamy midribs, is less vigorous, and does best with at least some shade.
Cultivars:
 'Beacon Silver': silver leaves with green edges; flowers pink; compact, grows 4-8″ (10-20cm).
 'Chequers': silver-variegated foliage and amethyst-violet flowers; height 9-12″ (23-30cm).
 'White Nancy': green-edged silver leaves often persist through winter; flowers white; height 6-8″ (15-20cm); spreads rapidly.
Zones: 3-10
Spacing: 15-18″ (38-45cm)
Propagation: seed, division

LATHYRUS (LATH-i-rus) ◯✕₩
Vetchling, Wild Pea
L. latifolius (la-ti-FOH-li-us)
Everlasting Pea, Perennial Sweet Pea
Vigorous flowering vine clings with tendrils. Best in rich, well-drained soil. Grow on fence or trellis, or where plants can scramble over stones or rocks. Showy rose-pink or white flowers open from summer to fall. Remove faded blossoms to extend season. Allow some seed-pods to develop for propagation. Tolerates some shade.
Zones: 3-10
Spacing: 18-24″ (45-60cm)
Propagation: seed

LAVANDULA (la-VAN-dew-la) ◯✕▲
L. angustifolia (an-goos-ti-FOH-li-a)
English Lavender
Bushy evergreen perennial with fragrant foliage and flowers. Best in moist, rich, yet well-drained soil. Useful in herb garden, border, or trimmed for low hedge. Semi-evergreen gray foliage topped by spikes of blue to purple flowers in summer. Flowers retain fragrance after drying. Mulch for winter protection in cold climates. Prune out older woody stems in spring to prevent overcrowding.
Zones: 5-10
Spacing: 15-18″ (38-45cm)
Propagation: division in early spring

Leontopodium alpinum

Liatris spicata

Liatris pycnostachya

LEONTOPODIUM (lee-on-to-POH-di-um) ○ ⋈

L. alpinum (al-PY-num)
Edelweiss

Gray-leaved alpine for dry rocky places. Height 6-12″ (15-30cm). Best in very well-drained, gritty alkaline soil. Useful for accent or mass planting, in rock garden or wall. Bright star-like flowers in summer are tiny yellow flower clusters surrounded by gray or white woolly bracts. Short-lived; intolerant of excess moisture.

Zones: 4-8
Spacing: 8-10″ (20-25cm)
Propagation: division, seed

LIATRIS (lee-AH-tris) ○ ◑ ⋉ N
Blazing-star, Gay-feather

Summer-blooming perennials with thickened, tuberous roots. Grow best in well-drained soil, planted 4-6″ (10-15cm) deep. Useful accent plants for border, container, and for cutting and drying. Purple or white flowers open from top of each stiffly erect spike.

Zones: 3-9
Spacing: 12-15″ (30-38cm)
Propagation: seed (species), division

L. pycnostachya (pik-noh-STAK-ee-a)
Kansas Gay-feather

Mauve or white flowers on feathery spikes. Grasslike foliage forms clump at base and clothes flowering stems. Height 3-5′ (0.9-1.5m). Heavy, 15-18″ (38-45cm) long flower spikes may need support. Intolerant of excess winter moisture.

L. scariosa (ska-ri-OH-sa)
Tall Gay-feather

White or purple varieties with fewer leaves on flowering stems. Height 2-4′ (0.6-1.2m). Hardy in zone 2.

L. spicata (spee-KAH-ta)
Spike Gay-feather

Mauve or white varieties, with attractive 6-15″ (15-38cm) spikes. Leaf size becomes progressively smaller up the flower stems. Height 24-36″ (60-90cm).

> Good drainage is essential for the majority of perennials. Roots in wet, sticky ground cannot breathe well, and the plants fail to thrive.

Ligularia przewalskii

Linum perenne

LIGULARIA (li-gew-LAH-ri-a) ○ ◑ ✂

Bold accents for moist, cool places. Prefer well-drained yet constantly moist, rich soil. Large, often decorative leaves. Mid- to late summer daisy-like flowers in loose clusters or tall spikes. Use baits to deter slugs and snails.

Zones: 4-8
Spacing: 24-36″ (60-90cm)
Propagation: division in spring, seed

L. dentata (den-TAH-ta)
Bigleaf Ligularia, Bigleaf Golden-ray
Long-stemmed, toothed leaves to 20″ (50cm) wide, useful for cut arrangements. Clusters of orange flowers.
Cultivar **'Desdemona'** has bronze foliage with purple undersides.

L. przewalski (sha-VAL-skee-y)
Shavalski's Ligularia
Deeply cut leaves, blackish stems, and tall narrow spikes of yellow blossoms. Height 4-6′ (1.2-1.8m).

L. stenocephala (sten-oh-KEF-a-la)
Narrow-spiked Ligularia
Coarsely toothed leaves, purplish stems, with bright yellow flowers in spikes that rise 4-6′ (1.2-1.8m).
Cultivar **'The Rocket'** has 18-24″ (45-60cm) spikes of lemon-yellow flowers.

LINUM (LY-num) ○
Flax

Reliable, clump-forming plants have feathery foliage and delicate yellow or blue flowers opening continuously from late spring or early summer. Best in light, well-drained soil. Useful in rock garden, at front of border, in natural planting. Tend to be short-lived but readily self-seed.

Zones: 4-9
Spacing: 12-18″ (30-45cm)
Propagation: seed, division

L. flavum (FLAH-vum)
Golden Flax
Big, loose clusters of 1″ (2.5cm) yellow flowers in summer. Height 12-24″ (30-60cm). Apply light winter mulch to protect near-woody stems.

L. narbonense (nar-boh-NEN-see)
Narbonne Flax
Slightly cup-shaped blue flowers in summer. Height 18-24″ (45-60cm). Cut stems back to about 8″ (20cm) after flowering, and apply mulch for winter protection in zone 5 and north.

L. perenne (pe-REN-nee)
Perennial Flax
Upright, dainty stems bear azure-blue flowers that open continuously from late spring. Tolerates partial shade, where flowering period can last 12 weeks. Height 12-18″ (30-45cm). Prune back after flowering to maintain attractive plant form.

Liriope muscari

Liriope spicata

Lobelia cardinalis

LIRIOPE (li-RY-oh-pay) ○ ◑ ● ∿ ⚶
Lilyturf

Spreading, mounding grass-like member of the lily family with clustered white or blue to purple flowers in summer. Thrives in any well-drained soil, sun or shade. Excellent as edging or low accent for border, or groundcover around trees and on slopes. Foliage may be damaged by ice and winds of northern winters.

Zones: see individual species
Spacing: 12-15″ (30-38cm)
Propagation: division

L. muscari (mus-KAH-ri)
Big Blue Lilytuft

Late summer flowers are white or shades of blue-purple. Dark berries persist into winter. Fleshy, strap-shaped leaves. Mounds 12-18″ (30-45cm). Zones 6-10. Grow lighter color flower and variegated leaf varieties with some shade.

L. spicata (spee-KAH-ta)
Creeping Lilytuft

Hardier species for zones 4-10. Summer flower spikes rise above mounded leaves to height of 8-12″ (20-30cm). Pale lilac or whitish blossom, blue-black berries.

LOBELIA (loh-BEE-li-a) ○ ◑ **N**

Vigorous perennials with brilliant summer flowers in colors that range from deep scarlet to dark blue. Prefer rich, moist yet well-drained soil; tolerate wet conditions. Good for accents, natural plantings. Tall clusters of tubular or star-like flowers on stiff stems. Lift and divide clumps every 3 years to maintain vigor. Often short-lived though self-seeding can perpetuate display. Apply protective mulch or lift and protect from northern winters.

Zones: 3-10
Spacing: 18-24″ (45-60cm)
Propagation: division, seed

L. cardinalis (kar-di-NAH-lis)
Cardinal Flower

Showy cardinal-red blossoms on 24″ (60cm) spikes rise to 2-4′ (0.6-1.2m). Foliage dark green or red-bronze.

L. siphilitica (si-fi-LIT-i-ka)
Great Lobelia, Blue Cardinal Flower

Blue flowered spikes rise to 24-36″ (60-90cm) in late summer. Leaves slightly downy. Grows well in moist, even boggy, soils.

Lunaria annua

Lupinus 'Russell Hybrids'

LUNARIA (loo-NAH-ri-a) ◐✂

L. annua (AN-ew-a)

[*L. biennis* (by-EN-is)]

Honesty, Silver-dollar Plant, Money Plant

Attractive, self-seeding biennial for use among perennials in partial shade. Thrives in any well-drained garden soil. Fragrant white to purple spring flowers are followed by unusual rounded, 2″ (5cm) paper-thin fruits, silvery when dry. Cut stems just as green color fades from fruit; hang to dry in cool airy place for 3-5 weeks.

Zones: 4-8

Spacing: 12-15″ (30-38cm)

Propagation: seed

Perennials whose bushy or tall growth is likely to flop over should be supported before this happens. Place small twiggy branches around the new growth of *Asters, Phlox,* and similar habit plants which can then grow upright through the supports. The flower stems of *Delphinium, Lupinus,* and hollyhocks *(Alcea)* will benefit from individual canes or light stakes, tied in several places so the weight of each flowering stem does not pull it down through a single high-placed tie.

LUPINUS (loo-PEEN-us) ○◐✂

Lupine

Vigorous though short-lived perennials valued for their colorful spring and summer flowers. Wild forms reseed in natural plantings. Good winter drainage essential.

Note: seeds and seedpods are poisonous.

Zones: 4-9

Spacing: 18-24″ (45-60cm)

Propagation: seed

Lupinus 'Russell Hybrids'

Showy perennials with colorful upright spikes of flowers. Height 3-4′ (0.9-1.2m). Good in mixed borders or for massed plantings. Prefer rich, moist yet well-drained, neutral to acid soil. Attractive mounds of grayish or bright green palmately lobed leaves. Densely packed, long flower clusters in clear white or shades of blue, purple, red, pink, cream, or yellow. Best where summer nights are cool.

L. perennis (pe-REN-nis) N

Wild Lupine

Deep-rooted wildflower with upright spikes of early summer blossom rising to about 24″ (60cm). Best in well-drained, acid, sandy soil; tolerates poor dry conditions. Good for nautural planting, borders. Flowers usually blue, sometimes pink or white.

Lychnis ✕ arkwrightii

Lysimachia nummularia

Lychnis chalcedonica

LYCHNIS (LIK-nis) ○ ✕
Campion, Catchfly
Upright plants with bright summer flowers. Good drainage essential
in cold areas. Useful in borders and natural landscapes where plants
readily self-seed.
Zones: 3-10
Spacing: 12-15″ (30-38cm)
Propagation: seed, division

L. ✕arkwrightii (ark-RYT-ee-y)
Arkwright's Campion
Brilliant orange-scarlet flowers are borne above dark bronze foliage.
Grows 18-24″ (45-60cm). Pinch early in the season to force addi-
tional shoots and reduce potential legginess.

L. chalcedonica (kal-se-DOH-ni-ka) N
Maltese-cross
Rounded clusters of small, deep scarlet, Maltese-cross-shaped flowers rise 24-36″ (60-90cm). Prefers consistent moisture. Dark green
leaves contrast well with flower color. Naturalized in North America.

L. viscaria (vis-KAH-ri-a)
German Catchfly
Magenta flower clusters top 12-18″ (30-45cm) plants in early summer. Tolerates dry conditions. Leafy tufts at base. Stems tend to be
sticky. Needs some shade in southern zones.

LYSIMACHIA (ly-si-MAH-ki-a) ○ ◐
Loosestrife
Vigorously spreading perennials with either upright or prostrate stems.
All prefer rich, moist, yet well-drained soils. Leaf margins smooth.
Flowers rounded or bell-shaped, borne singly or narrow spikes.
Zones: 3-8
Spacing: 12-24″ (30-60cm)
Propagation: division, seed

L. clethroides (kleth-ROI-deez) ✕
Gooseneck Loosestrife
Spreading clump has white late summer flowers on slender, arching
spikes. Useful in natural planting; frequent division contains exuberant spread in formal border. Height 24-36″ (60-90cm).

L. nummularia (nu-mew-LAH-ri-a) ⤳ N
Creeping Jennie, Moneywort, Creeping Charlie
Rapidly spreading, naturalized creeper mounds 4-8″ (10-20cm) high.
Grows well in moist or wet conditions. Good groundcover near
streams, pools. Smoothly rounded leaves. Bright yellow fragrant flowers in early summer. Cultivar **'Aurea'** (AW-ree-a) has yellow leaves.

Lythrum salicaria

Macleaya cordata

LYSIMACHIA (cont'd) ✕ N

L. punctata (punk-TAH-ta)
Yellow Loosestrife
Lemon-yellow blossoms open in early summer on stiffly erect flowering spikes. Height 12-24″ (30-60cm). Tolerates either wet or dry soil. Best in partial shade. Naturalized.

LYTHRUM (LITH-rum) ○ ◑ N

Lythrum, Loosestrife
Upright, clump-forming perennials for moist locations. Useful in borders and natural plantings. Small summer flowers in pink or purple, clustered onto long 4-angled stems. Naturalized. Several named cultivars offer variety of color and height.
Zones: 3-9
Spacing: 15-18″ (38-45cm)
Propagation: division

L. salicaria (sa-li-KAH-ri-a)
Purple Lythrum or **Loosestrife**
Willow-like leaves and rose-purple flowers. Height 3-5′ (0.9-1.5m). Tolerates heat and humidity.

L. virgatum (vir-GAH-tum)
Purple Loosestrife
Smaller plant grows to 24-36″ (60-90cm). Purple flowers.

MACLEAYA (mak-LAY-a) ○

M. cordata (kor-DAH-ta)
Plume Poppy
Handsome large perennial grows 5-10′ (1.5-3.0m) tall. Best in rich, well-drained soil. Useful accent specimen with attractive foliage and feathery summer flowers; or plant as background in border display. Broad, lobed gray-green leaves have silvery undersides. Creamy-white plumes of blossom are 10-12″ (25-30cm) long. Spreads vigorously.
Zones: 3-10
Spacing: 3-4′ (0.9-1.2m)
Propagation: division, root cuttings, seed

Marrubium vulgare

Malva moschata

Melissa officinalis

Malva alcea

MALVA (MAL-va) ○ ◑ N
Mallow
Informal, free-flowering perennials naturalized in North America. Prefer dry, alkaline soil; in warmer areas, plant in deeper, richer soil. Useful in mixed borders, self-seeding in natural plantings. Flowers white or pink, summer and early fall. Short-lived plants easily grown from seed.
Zones: 4-9
Spacing: 12″ (30cm)
Propagation: seed, division

M. alcea (al-SEE-a)
Hollyhock Mallow
Loose clusters of rose to white flowers. Grows 24-36″ (60-90cm) tall. Light green foliage.
Cultivar **'Fastigiata'** (fa-sti-gi-AH-ta) has 2″ (5cm) rose-pink flowers on more upright, well-branched plant; height 3-4′ (0.9-1.2m).

M. moschata (mos-KAH-ta)
Musk Mallow
Symmetrical, shrubby plants grow about 36″ (90cm) tall. Dark green feathery foliage and rose or white flowers.

MARRUBIUM (ma-ROO-bi-um) ○ N
M. vulgare (vul-GAH-ree)
Horehound, Hoarhound
Vigorous, spreading herb grows 18-30″ (45-75cm) high. Velvety, down-covered foliage and stems used to flavor medicines, tea, candy. Grows in any well-drained soil. Naturalized member of the Mint family.
Zones: 3-10
Spacing: 10″ (25cm)
Propagation: seed, division

MELISSA (me-LIS-a) ○ ◑ N
M. officinalis (o-fi-si-NAH-lis)
Lemon Balm
Rapidly spreading herb grows 24-36″ (60-90cm) high. Light, dry soils enhance flavor. Lemon-scented leaves used in teas, soups, to season veal and poultry, and in toiletries. Small white flowers cluster in leaf axils on square stems. Naturalized member of the Mint family.
Zones: 4-10
Spacing: 18″ (45cm)
Propagation: seed, divisions, cuttings

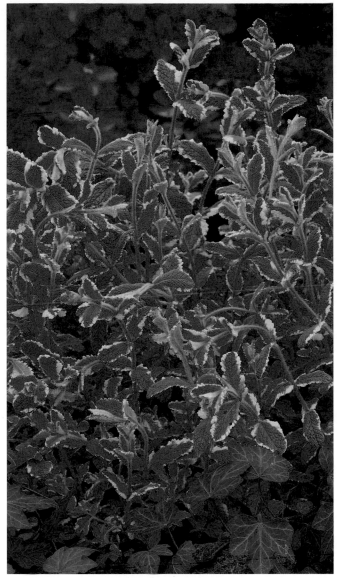

Mentha suaveolens

Mertensia virginica

MENTHA   (MEN-tha) ○◑
Mint
Spreading herbs with square stems and small blue, pink, or white flowers. Best in rich, moist, slightly acid soil. May become invasive.
Zones: 4-10
Spacing: 12-15″ (30-38cm)
Propagation: division

M. × piperita   (py-pe-REE-ta)
Peppermint
Height 12-24″ (30-60cm). Reddish-green stems, fragrant leaves, and dense spikes of violet flowers in late summer.

M. pulegium   (poo-LEG-i-um) ⤳
Pennyroyal
Aromatic groundcover with creeping stems and spikes of lavender-blue or pink summer flowers. Height 18-24″ (45-60cm). Bitter-tasting leaves and stems have been used in medicines, puddings, sauces. Hardy only to zone 7.

M. suaveolens   (swah-vee-OH-lenz) **N**
[*M. rotundifolia*   (roh-tun-di-FOH-li-a)]
Apple Mint, Pineapple Mint
Height 6-36″ (15-90cm). Rounded, wrinkled, downy, 1-4″ (2.5-10cm) leaves. Grayish-white flower clusters become pink or violet. Naturalized.

M. spicata   (spee-KAH-ta) **N**
Spearmint
Strongest mint, used to flavor teas, sauces, jellies, salads, vegetables, and in cooking meats. Height 12-24″ (30-60cm). Dense spikes of violet or pink flowers rise above green foliage. Naturalized.

MERTENSIA   (mer-TEN-zi-a) ◑● **N**
M. virginica   (vir-JIN-i-ka)
Virginia Bluebells
Spring-blooming, summer dormant perennial has nodding clusters of blue, bell-shaped flowers. Height 12-24″ (30-60cm). Prefers rich, acid, moist soil. Grow in shady border, woodland or natural garden. Gray-green oval leaves. Flower buds pink, turning blue as they open and mature.
Zones: 3-9
Spacing: 15-18″ (38-45cm)
Propagation: seed

Miscanthus sinensis 'Zebrinus'

Miscanthus sinensis 'Variegatus'

Molinia caerulea 'Variegata'

MISCANTHUS (miz-KAN-thus) ○ ◑ ⚥
Silver Grass
Large, upright, clump-forming ornamental grasses for accent, screen. Best in deep, fertile soil that has plenty of available moisture but is not soggy. Leaf blades have white midribs, rough margins. Flowers in feathery-looking flat or fan-shaped panicles. Cut top growth back in late winter.
Zones: 5-10: see individual species
Spacing: 2-5′ (0.6-1.5m), depending on species
Propagation: division in spring

M. sinensis (sy-NEN-sis)
Japanese Silver Grass, Eulalia Grass
Dense clumps of cascading foliage grow to 7′ (2.1m) high. Tolerates moisture; suitable for waterside planting. Most forms hardy in zone 4. Fan-shaped flower clusters open red, become white with age, remain attractive through winter. Winter foliage almond or buff color. Clump centers die out with age.
Cultivars and varieties:
  'Gracillimus', Maiden Grass: slender, dark green leaf blades; clump grows to 5′ (1.5m); leaf-tips curl in fall.
  'Variegatus' (ve-ri-e-GAH-tus), **Variegated Silver Grass:** graceful white-and-green striped leaves; height to 4′ (1.2m); hardy in zones 5 and 6 only; needs partial shade.

  'Zebrinus' (zee-BRY-nus), **Zebra Grass:** bright green foliage has yellow stripes across the blades; narrow, upright clump to 7′ (2.1m); leaves have rusty-orange tips in winter.
  'Silberfeder', Silverfeather Grass: medium green foliage and large silvery-white plumes of flowers in summer.
  M. s. var. *condensatus* (kon-den-SAY-tus): dense clump grows to 5-6′(1.5-1.8m); broad, flat, white-ribbed leaves. Flower cluster opens burgundy becoming bronze in winter.
  M. s. var. *purpurascens* (pur-pew-RAS-enz), **Purpurascens Silver Grass:** Smaller, upright variety grows 3-4′(0.9-1.2m) tall; broad, dark green leaf blades. Flowers with silvery-white plumes in late summer. Whole plant turns brilliant red-orange in fall.

MOLINIA (moh-LIN-i-a) ○ ◑ ⚥
M. caerulea (se-REW-lee-a)
Purple Moor Grass
Adaptable ornamental grass grows in tall, narrow tufts. Height 2-4′ (0.6-1.2m). Useful in borders and as accent. Best in moist, well-drained, acid soil. Blue-gray leaves. Purplish flower clusters (panicles) in summer. Cultivar **'Variegata'** (ve-ri-e-GAH-ta) has yellow-striped green leaves.
Zones: 5-10
Spacing: 15-24″ (38-60cm)
Propagation: division

Monarda didyma

Myosotis sylvatica

Monarda didyma

MONARDA (moh-NAR-da) ◐◑✕ N
Wild Bergamot, Horsemint
Aromatic ornamental herbs with dense terminal clusters of white, red, purplish, or yellow flowers surrounded by colorful bracts. Grow rapidly in rich, moist soil. Useful spreaders for natural planting, accent in border. Mint family. Sometimes used to mask odors in oils, perfumes.
Zones: 4-9: see individual species
Spacing: 12-15″ (30-38cm)
Propagation: division

M. didyma (DID-i-ma)
Bee Balm
Summer flowers are red, pink, or white, attracting bees, hummingbirds, butterflies. Height 2-4′ (0.6-1.2m).
Cultivar **'Cambridge Scarlet'** is very vigorous, with flaming scarlet flowers.

M. fistulosa (fis-tew-LOH-sa)
Wild Bergamot
Lavender flowers with whitish or purple bracts on 2-4′ (0.6-1.2m) plants. Hardy to zone 3.

MYOSOTIS (my-o-SOH-tis) ◐◑
Forget-me-not, Scorpion Grass
Short-lived, self-seeding perennial forms clumps 6-18″ (15-45cm) high. Best in moist, well-drained soils. Useful in rock gardens, on shaded banks, in woodland and natural plantings. Small clear-blue spring to early summer flowers open in slightly coiled clusters resembling scorpion tails.
Zones: 3-9
Spacing: 9-12″ (23-30cm)
Propagation: seed, division

M. alpestris (al-PES-tris) N
Alpine Forget-me-not
Small tufted plant grows to about 6″ (15cm).

M. scorpioides (skor-pi-OI-deez) N
Water Forget-me-not
Naturalized species mounds 10-20″ (25-50cm). Best in moist or boggy soils, beside stream, pond.

M. sylvatica (sil-VAT-i-ka)
Woodland Forget-me-not
Self-seeding annual or biennial species. Blue, pink, or white flowers. Best with some shade. Soft, hairy leaves.

Nepeta cataria

Nierembergia repens

Oenothera missouriensis

NEPETA (NEP-e-ta) ○ ◑ ⋈
Catmint

Spreading aromatic herbs with gray-green leaves topped by spikes of clustering late spring flowers. Grow rapidly in rich, moist soils. Contain vigor with sandy, drier conditions. Useful as edging, in rock or herb gardens, natural plantings. Mint family.

Zones: 3-8
Spacing: 12-18″ (30-45cm)
Propagation: seed, division

N. cataria (ka-TAH-ri-a) **N**
Catnip

Height 24-36″ (60-90cm). Lemon-minty scent of crushed leaves delights cats. Used in teas. Flowers pale pink to white. Naturalized.

N. × faassenii (fah-SEN-ee-y)
Persian Ground Ivy, Persian Catmint

Bushy plant mounds 12-18″ (30-45cm). Tolerates dry soil. Pale-blue flowers in early summer. Trim off dead blooms to encourage second flowering.

NIEREMBERGIA (nee-rem-BER-ji-a) ○ ◑ ⋈
Cupflower

N. repens (REE-pens)
Whitecup, White Cupflower

Spreading tender perennial has delicate white, purple or rose-tinted summer flowers. Forms mat 2-4″ (5-10cm) high. Best in moist, well-drained soil. Useful edging and bedding plant, in rock gardens, between paving stones. Remove dead flowers and cut back in fall to encourage fresh spring growth. Mulch for winter protection. Grow as annual north of zone 7.

Zones: 7-10
Spacing: 6-12″ (15-30cm)
Propagation: seed, division

OENOTHERA (ee-no-THEE-ra) ○ ◑ **N**
Evening Primrose, Sundrops

Spreading, often shrubby perennials with showy paper-thin flowers in summer. Most are yellow, and many open in the evening. Thrive in well-drained, sandy soil.

Zones: see individual species
Spacing: 12-15″ (30-45cm)
Propagation: division, seed, cuttings

Oenothera speciosa

Origanum vulgare

Oenothera tetragona

Osmunda claytoniana

OENOTHERA (cont'd)

O. fruticosa (froo-ti-KOH-sa)
Sundrops
Bright yellow blossoms open in terminal clusters on reddish, slender stems. Height 18-24″ (45-60cm). Good border plant. Prefers dry soil. Zones 4-9.

O. missouriensis (mi-zoor-ri-EN-sis)
Ozark Sundrops, Missouri Primrose
Spreading plant produces series of large, fragrant, 5″ (13cm) bright yellow flowers. Each blossom lasts from evening to end of next day. Reddish growing tips turn upward. Height 6-12″ (15-30cm). Useful groundcover for poor soils and full sun. Zones 4-9.

O. speciosa (spee-si-OH-sa)
White or **Showy Evening Primrose**
Vigorous species for natural plantings, especially in warmer humid climates. Height 12-24″ (30-60cm). Fragrant white flowers open during day, turn rose-pink with age. Plants often short-lived, self-seeding in good conditions. Zones 5-9.

O. tetragona (tet-ra-GOH-na)
Four-angled Sundrops
Clusters of lemon-yellow flowers open at night in late spring. Good border plant. Height 12-36″ (30-60cm). Reddish-brown stems, well-branched plant, growing tips red. Short-lived perennial often treated as biennial. Zones 5-9.

ORIGANUM (o-RIG-a-num) ◯ N

O. vulgare (vul-GAH-ree)
Dittany, Marjoram, Oregano
Aromatic herb forms spreading, trailing mat. Height to 18″ (45cm). Best in well-drained neutral to alkaline soil. Good container, edging, herb garden plant. Older stems become woody. Clusters of tiny mauve flowers in summer. Leaves useful as culinary flavoring; plant parts also used medicinally. Naturalized.
Zones: 3-10
Spacing: 8-15″ (20-38cm)
Propagation: seed, division, cuttings

OSMUNDA (oz-MUN-da) ◖● N

O. claytoniana (klay-to-nee-AH-na)
Interrupted Fern
Hardy deciduous fern for moist, shady location. Height 24-36″ (60-90cm). Best in acid soil. Pale green foliage, outer sterile fronds larger than inner fertile ones.
Zones: 4-9
Spacing: 18-24″ (45-60cm)
Propagation: division, spores (sow as soon as ripe)

Pachysandra terminalis

Paeonia suffriticosa

Paeonia lactiflora

Paeonia lactiflora

PACHYSANDRA (pa-ki-SAN-dra) ◐●〜♠
P. terminalis (ter-mi-NAH-lis)
Japanese Spurge

Evergreen, stoloniferous groundcover for shaded areas. Height 9-12″ (23-30cm) high. Prefers moist, well-drained soil; tolerates dry conditions. Plant in shade of trees, fence, building. Leaves dark glossy green, turn yellow in hot sun. Spikes of white flowers in late spring. Cultivars:

   'Green Carpet': compact, darker green form, 6-8″ (15-20cm) high.
   'Silveredge': light green leaves with narrow silvery-white margins.
   'Variegata' (ve-ri-e-GAH-ta): white variegations; less vigorous form
    needs shade to prevent scorching.

Zones: 4-9
Spacing: 6-12″ (15-30cm)
Propagation: division, cuttings

Plant perennials with weed-free rootstocks, and keep them as weed-free as possible. Once weeds become established among close-knit perennial roots, it is almost impossible to remove them without destroying the specimens.

PAEONIA (pe-OH-ni-a) ○◐✂
Peony

Reliable, long-lived hardy herbaceous perennials or deciduous shrubs with huge showy blooms from late spring to early summer. Thrive in rich, well-drained soil. Fine in borders, as hedge, or accents in front of shrubs, wall, or fence. Compound leaves.

Zones: 3-8
Spacing: 2-4′ (0.6-1.2m)
Propagation: seed, division (herbaceous), cuttings (shrub)

P. lactiflora (lak-ti-FLOH-ra)
Chinese Peony, Common Garden Peony

Herbaceous, spreading clumps of erect, arching stems form mounds 2-4′ (0.6-1.2m) high. Flowers single, semi-double, double, and anemone-form. Colors white, shades of pink, purple, red, and sometimes yellow. New shoots red; protect against late freezes. Stake to support tall plants and large blooms. Plant with crown (red buds visible in fall) 1-2″ (2.5-5cm) deep.

P. suffruticosa (suf-roo-ti-KOH-sa)
Tree Peony

Deciduous shrub grows 4-6′ (1.2-1.8m) tall. Prefers partial shade. Tolerates moist soils. Useful in perennial or shrub border. Large flowers 6-10″ (15-25cm) across, single or semi-double, in white and shades of pink, purple, and red. Characteristic fuzzy fruits. Slow growing. Flower colors fade in full sun.

Papaver orientale

Papaver orientale

Pennisetum alopecuroides

PAPAVER (pa-PAH-vur) ○
Poppy
Showy and colorful cup-shaped flowers rise singly on long flower stems above lobed or finely dissected foliage. Best in moist, well-drained soil. Must have good winter drainage. Characteristic milky sap.
Zones: 2-8: see individual species
Spacing: 15-18″ (38-45cm)
Propagation: seed, division in late summer

P. burseri (BUR-se-ry)
[P. alpinum (al-PY-num)]
Alpine Poppy
Self-seeding perennial for rock garden or edging use in zones 4-7. Height 8-10″ (20-25cm). Semi-evergreen, gray-green, finely divided foliage. Silky, fragrant summer flowers in white, yellow, and pink. Short-lived perennial easily grown from seed. Intolerant of heat.

P. nudicaule (new-di-KAW-lee) ◑ ↝
Iceland Poppy, Arctic Poppy
Tufting perennial with fragrant spring flowers, for rock garden, edging, groundcover, front of border. Height 12-18″ (30-45cm). Gray-green lobed foliage. Silky flowers yellow, greenish, orange, pink, red. Flowers first year from seed. Short-lived.

P. orientale (o-ree-en-TAH-lee)
Oriental Poppy
Flamboyant scarlet, pink, or white early summer blossoms have dark centers and purple-black marking at petal base. Height 18-36″. Good in mixed borders, natural plantings, so other plants can fill in when poppies become dormant. Strong green leaves die back in summer. Divide clumps every 4-6 years. Plant with crowns about 3″ deep. New foliage often grows in fall. Mulch for winter protection.

PENNISETUM (pen-i-SEE-tum) ○ ✕ ↯
Fountain Grass
P. alopecuroides (a-loh-pek-ew-ROI-deez)
Chinese Fountain Grass, Rose F. G.
Compact ornamental grass forming dense, 24-36″ (60-90cm) mounds of graceful, arching bright green foliage. Useful border accent. Needs well-drained, fertile soil. Flowers in summer; pinkish-white plumes mature to rose-copper seedheads, good in dried arrangements.
Cultivar **'Hameln'** is small form, growing to 18″ (45cm).
Zones: 5-10
Spacing: 24″ (60cm)
Propagation: division, seed

Penstemon digitalis 'Husker Red'

Perovskia atriplicifolia

Penstemon barbatus

Petrorhagia saxifraga

PENSTEMON (pen-STEE-mon) ◐ N
Beard-tongue
Showy perennial best in moist, well-drained soil. Useful for middle to back of borders, natural plantings, smaller varieties for rock gardens. Nodding, tubular flowers in open spikes. Easily grown from seed.
Zones: 2-8
Spacing: 12-18″ (30-45cm)
Propagation: seed, division, cuttings

P. barbatus (bar-BAH-tus)
Beardlip Penstemon, Common Beard-tongue
Semi-evergreen. Spring flowers pink or rose, in long narrow racemes that open from the bottom. Height 18-36″ (45-60cm).
Cultivars:
   'Crystal': white flowers; grows 18-24″ (30-60cm).
   'Pinifolius': orange-scarlet flowers, pine-like foliage; grows 8″ (20cm).
   'Prairie Dawn': pale pink flowers.
   'Prairie Fire': deep red flowers; grows to 24″ (60cm).

P. digitalis (di-ji-TAH-lis)
White Penstemon
Erect plant with purplish stems, grows 3-5′ (0.9-1.5m) tall. Early summer flowers are white or pink, in loose clusters.
Cultivar **'Husker Red'** has red leaves and stems, with white flowers tinged pink; height 30-34″ (75-85cm).

PEROVSKIA (pe-ROV-ski-a) ○
P. atriplicifolia (a-tri-pli-si-FOH-li-a)
Azure Sage, Russian Sage
Shrubby, aromatic, gray-green sage with pale blue summer flowers. Grows 3-5′ (0.9-1.5m) tall. Prefers very well-drained soil. Useful border plant, in blue-gray groupings, with ornamental grasses, as low hedge or screen. Cut back to 12-18″ (30-45cm) after first hard frost in fall. Loses upright form when grown with shade.
Zones: 5-9
Spacing: 24-36″ (60-90cm)
Propagation: cuttings in summer, seed

PETRORHAGIA (pet-ro-RAH-gi-a) ○ ↬
P. saxifraga (sak-SIF-ra-ga)
[*Tunica saxifraga* (TEW-ni-ka)]
Tunic Flower, Coat Flower
Compact, spreading perennial forms mat 4″ (10cm) high. Best in poor, dry soils. Good edging, cover for rocky banks. Tufts of bristly, grass-like leaves on thin, wiry stems. White to pale purple summer flowers. Self-seeding.
Zones: 3-9
Spacing: 6-10″ (15-25cm)
Propagation: seed

Phalaris arundinacea var. picta

Phlox divaricata

Phlox stolonifera

PHALARIS (fa-LAH-ris) ○ ✔
Canary Grass
P. arundinacea* var. *picta (a-run-din-AY-see-a PIK-ta)
Ribbon Grass, Gardener's-garters
Vigorous ornamental grass has bright green-and-white arching foliage.
Height 24-36″ (60-90cm). Useful in borders, as accent. Thrives in
any fertile soil. Tolerates moist conditions; suitable for planting close
to water. Narrow clusters of flowers open in summer. Leaf color fades
in hot sun. Tolerates poorer soils and some shade with reduced vigor.
Zones: 4-10
Spacing: 24″ (60cm)
Propagation: division

PHLOX (FLOKS) N
Useful group of perennials provides bright flowers for most garden
situations. Phlox grow best in well-drained soils. Stiff, sometimes woo-
dy, upright or prostrate stems bear lance-shaped or needle-like leaves.
Clear flowers; colors range from white to pink to blue and purple,
often with contrasting centers (eyes).
Zones: 3-9
Spacing: 12-18″ (30-45cm): see individual species
Propagation: seed, cuttings, division

P. divaricata (dy-va-ri-KAH-ta) ◑ ➻
Wild Blue Phlox
Semi-evergreen spreader with open clusters of fragrant blue spring
flowers. Height 12-15″ (30-38cm). Good edging for shaded, moist
yet well-drained sites.
Cultivar **'Fuller's White'** has white flowers and grows to 8-12″
(20-30cm); tolerates some sun.
P. d.* var. *laphamii (lap-HAY-mee-y) has dark blue flowers.

P. maculata (ma-kew-LAH-ta) ○
Wild Sweet William
Showy clusters of early summer flowers are mauve-pink, purple, or
white. Height 24-36″ (60-90cm). Good in border or natural planting.
Thick, glossy dark green leaves, red-mottled stems.
Cultivars:
  'Alpha': flowers rose-pink with darker eye.
  'Miss Lingard': pure white flowers in late spring.
  'Omega': masses of white flowers with lilac eye.

Phlox paniculata

Phlox subulata

Phlox maculata 'Omega'

Physalis alkekengi

PHLOX (cont'd)

P. paniculata (pa-ni-kew-LAH-ta) ○ ✕
Border Phlox, Garden Phlox

Fragrant summer flowers are magenta, red, purple, pink, or white, in large dense pyramidal clusters. Height 3-4' (0.9-1.2m). Good for massed plantings or for accents in border. Needs some shade in hot dry climates. Tolerates moist soils. To help avoid powdery mildew infection, space at 24" (60cm) or more for better air circulation.

P. stolonifera (stoh-lo-NIF-e-ra) ◑ ⚬ ▲
Creeping Phlox

Low spreader forms dense cover 6-12" (15-30cm) high. Useful for shaded edging, rock garden. Very early spring flowers, violet to lavender. Cultivars:
  'Blue Ridge': blue-lilac flowers.
  'Bruce's White': flowers white with yellow eye.

P. subulata (soo-bew-LAH-ta) ○ ⚬ ▲
Moss Phlox, Moss Pink

Spreading mounds covered with flowers in early spring. Height 6-9" (15-23cm). Best in sunny, well-drained sandy soil. Good edging, container, rock garden plant. Stiff, needlelike foliage on woody stems.

PHYSALIS (FY-sa-lis) ○ ◑ ✕
Ground Cherry, Husk Tomato

P. alkekengi (al-ke-KEN-gi)
[*P. franchetii* (fran-KET-ee-y)]
Chinese-lantern

Spreading perennial has ornamental orange seed-pods. Height 18-24" (45-60cm). Grows in any garden soil. Best in informal grouping. Oval foliage tends to hide small creamy-white summer flowers. Red fruit are encased in bright orange lantern-like calyces that lose color when left on plants. For drying, cut stems as leaves begin to die back; hang to dry in cool airy place for 3-5 weeks. Can be grown as an annual.

Zones: 3-10
Spacing: 24" (60cm)
Propagation: seed, division in spring

When perennial growth slows and foliage starts to yellow and dry, reduce watering frequency even in dry climates. Don't stop watering altogether until plants are dormant--roots and stems below ground continue to develop and, in many cases, to store food for next season's growth.

Physostegia virginiana 'Summer Snow'

Physostegia virginiana

Platycodon grandiflorus

PHYSOSTEGIA (fy-so-STEE-ji-a) ○ ◐ ✕ N
P. virginiana (vir-ji-nee-AH-na)
Obedience, False Dragonhead
Slender, upright perennial topped with spikes of pink to purple late summer flowers. Height 3-4′ (0.9-1.2m). Prefers moist, acid, well-drained soil and full sun; tolerates drier soil with some shade. Good in border, natural planting. Heavy flowering stems need support. Divide clumps every 2-3 years. Spreads vigorously; may become invasive. Cultivars:

    'Nana' (NAH-na): dwarf form grows to 12-18″ (30-45cm).
    'Summer Snow': flowers white; spreads less aggressively.
    'Vivid': vibrant pink flowers; height 24-36″ (60-90cm).
Zones: 2-9
Spacing: 15-18″ (38-45cm)
Propagation: seed, division

PLATYCODON (pla-ti-KOH-don) ○
P. grandiflorus (gran-di-FLOH-rus)
Balloon Flower
Reliable, perennial emerges late in spring and blooms all summer. Height 30-36″ (75-90cm). Best in moist, well-drained soil. Provides good summer color in border or as accent. Oval, serrated leaves. Bell-shaped flowers open from inflated balloon-like buds. Blue-purple varieties best in full sun; pinks and whites tolerate some shade. Clumps do not spread and can remain undisturbed.
P. g.* var. *mariesii (ma-REE-zee-y), **Dwarf Balloon Flower,** is compact, grows to 12-24″ (30-60cm); useful for edging or rock garden.
Zones: 3-8
Spacing: 12-18″ (30-45cm)
Propagation: seed, division in spring

During their first season, water perennials when the soil begins to dry. Early morning is the best time to water. Apply it at ground level, giving enough to soak around the young roots and encourage them to grow more deeply into the prepared soil.

Polemonium caeruleum

Polygonatum commutatum

POLEMONIUM (po-le-MOH-ni-um) ◐

Clump-forming perennials with informal, branching clusters of white, blue or purple flowers. Best in well-drained soil. Prefer cooler climates. Useful in partly shaded borders, at edge of woodland. Delicate, apple green leaflets arranged ladder-like on stems.

Zones: 2-8
Spacing: 18″ (45cm)
Propagation: seed, division in fall

P. caeruleum (se-REW-lee-um) ✂
Jacob's-ladder, Greek Valerian

Summer flowers light to deep blue with yellow stamens. Height 18-36″ (45-90cm).

P. reptans (REP-tans) ⤳ N
Creeping Jacob's-ladder

Spring flowers in shades of pale blue. Height to 12″ (30cm).

POLYGONATUM (po-li-go-NAH-tum) ◐ ● ✂ N
Solomon's-seal

Rhizomatous plants with long, gracefully curving stems. Grow well in shady, moist, acid soil. Useful for damp woodlands, among shrubs, bulbs, in shaded borders and natural plantings. Handsome foliage for cut arrangements. Whitish bell-shaped late spring flowers hang below leaf nodes. Shining dark berries in fall.

Zones: 3-9
Spacing: 12-15″ (30-38cm)
Propagation: seed, division .

P. biflorum (by-FLOH-rum)
Small Solomon's-seal

Height 24-36″ (60-90cm). Leaves about 4″ (10cm) long on arching stems. Yellowish-white flowers.

P. commutatum (ko-mew-TAH-tum)
Great Solomon's-seal

Species for large-scale informal plantings. Height 3-7′ (0.9-2.1m). Flowers yellow- or whitish-green.

P. odoratum (oh-do-RAH-tum)
Solomon's-seal

Sweetly fragrant flowers are white with greenish markings. Height 18-24″ (45-60cm).

Polygonum aubertii

Polygonum cuspidatum var. *compactum*

POLYGONUM (po-LIG-o-num) ○ ⋙
Knotweed, Smartweed, Fleece Flower

Densely spreading, often evergreen clump-forming groundcovers and deciduous woody vines. Grow well in moist soils. Vigorous growth. Numerous small flowers cluster in tight spikes or in loose, feathery panicles. May become invasive.

Zones: 4-8
Spacing: 18-24″ (45-60cm)
Propagation: seed, division, cuttings

Polygonum cultivars:

'Border Jewel': compact leafy clumps grow to about 4″ (10cm) high. Useful groundcover for edging. Dark green foliage turns bright red in fall. Small spikes of light pink flowers.

'Superbum' (soo-PER-bum): clump-forming spreader with big paddle-like lower leaves. Height 24-36″ (60-90cm). Good groundcover selections from *P. bistorta* (bis-TOR-ta). Dense 6″ (15cm) spikes of pink flowers in early summer; may bloom again in late summer.

P. aubertii (aw-BER-tee-y)
Silver Fleece Vine, Silver-lace Vine

Twining, deciduous woody vine can grow 20-40′ (6-12m) in one season. Makes dense cover on fence or rocky bank. Profuse clusters of scented, fluffy white flowers in mid-summer.

P. cuspidatum (kus-pi-DAH-tum)
Japanese Knotweed, Japanese Fleece Flower

Large and very vigorous rhizomatous spreader with clumps rising to 6-8′ (1.8-2.4m). Use in large-scale informal and natural plantings. Stems hollow and jointed. Numerous greenish-white flower clusters in late summer.

P. c.* var. *compactum (kom-PAK-tum): smaller form grows to 24″ (60cm). Useful vigorous groundcover for boggy or moist places. Pink or pinkish-red flowers. May be sold as *P. reynoutria* (ray-NOO-tri-a).

Potentilla tabernaemontani var. nana

Potentilla atrosanguinea 'Gibson Scarlet'

Potentilla napalensis 'Miss Willmott'

POTENTILLA (poh-ten-TIL-a) ○ ◑
Cinquefoil, Five-finger
Mounding, clumping, often herbaceous perennials with loose clusters of rose-like flowers in spring or summer. Best in light, sandy soil and where nights are cool. Useful in borders, some as groundcover and in rock gardens. Stems erect or sprawling.
Zones: 5-8
Spacing: 12-15″ (30-38cm)
Propagation: division, seed

P. atrosanguinea (at-roh-san-GWIN-ee-a)
Himalayan Cinquefoil
Summer-flowering potentilla mounds 18-30″ (45-70cm). Prefers full sun. Three-parted leaves are silky-hairy. Deep red flowers.
Cultivar **'Gibson Scarlet'** has blood-red flowers and soft green foliage; grows to 18″ (45cm).

P. nepalensis (ne-pa-LEN-sis)
Nepal Cinquefoil
Vigorous growth to 18-24″ (45-60cm). Rosy-purple summer flowers. Leaves up to 12″ (30cm) long. To maintain form, trim back severely after flowering.
Cultivar **'Miss Willmott'** ['Willmottiae' (wil-MOT-ee-y)]: compact form grows 10-12″ (25-30cm); carmine flowers have cherry-red centers.

P. tabernaemontani (ta-ber-nee-mon-TAH-ni) ↬
Spring Cinquefoil
[*P. verna* (VER-na)]
Spreading, rooting stems form mat 6-9″ (15-23cm) high. Spring flowers yellow. Rhizomatous.
P. t.* var. *nana (NAH-na): dwarf form grows to 3-4″ (8-10cm), has golden-yellow flowers.

> When bulb flowers have faded, cut off the flowers but not the whole green stems, so that the plants' strength is directed toward developing strong bulbs for next season's display. Once flowering has stopped, foliage clusters can be neatened by tying small groups into loose knots until they, too, have faded.

Primula japonica

Primula vulgaris

Primula vulgaris

PRIMULA (PRIM-ew-la) ○ ✂
Primrose

Colorful and fragrant spring-flowering perennials for borders, rock gardens, containers, massed or natural plantings. All form clumps that will spread in good conditions. Best in partial shade though some tolerate full sun and/or deep shade. Flowers borne in clusters on erect, leafless stems above or among leafy rosettes.

Zones: 3-8
Spacing: 6-12″ (15-30cm)
Propagation: seed, division

P. auricula (aw-RIK-ew-la)
Auricula Primrose

Fragrant blossoms rise to 6-9″(15-23cm). Species yellow, varieties offer wide range of color. Prefer well-drained, alkaline soil in sun or shade. Basal leaves often evergreen.

P. denticulata (den-ti-kew-LAH-ta)
Drumstick Primrose

Characteristic globular lilac or white flower clusters top 10-20″ (25-50cm) slender stems. Best in moist, well-drained soils and partial shade. If grown in sun, do not allow soil to dry out. After flowering, leaves grow longer, to about 12″ (30cm) long.

P. japonica (ja-PON-i-ka)
Japanese Primrose

Bold, upright clumps for cool, moist to boggy soil. Best in acid, peaty conditions in partial shade or sun: do not allow soil to dry in sun. Leaves 6-12″ (15-30cm). Several flower colors, with clusters encircling 12-24″ (30-60cm) stems in several places.

P. ×polyantha (po-lee-AN-tha)
Polyantha Primrose

Shortlived hybrids with flat- or round-topped clusters of bloom. Often grown as annual or biennial bedding plants. Height 8-12″ (20-30cm). Grow in well-drained soil; tolerates sun when soil does not dry out. Leaves dark green. Many colorful selections.

P. sieboldii (see-BOHL-dee-y)
Siebold Primrose, Japanese Star Primrose

Late spring primrose for both full sun and deep shade. Prefers moist, peat-acid soil and shade; tolerates some soil drying. Downy plants grow 4-8″ (10-20cm) high. Heart-shaped leaves on long stems. Flowers usually purple with white eyes; may also be white or rose. Summer dormant.

P. vulgaris (vul-GAH-ris)
English Primrose

Yellow or shades of blue to purple flowers often have darker centers. Height 6-9″ (15-23cm). Best in moist, well-drained soil. Tolerates sun if soil does not dry out.

Pulmonaria saccharata

Pulsatilla vulgaris

Ranunculus repens

PULMONARIA (pul-mo-NAH-ri-a) ◑
Lungwort
Low, spreading perennials for edging, front of shaded border, among bulbs. Spring flowers open with or before new foliage. Best in moist, well-drained soil. Lance-shaped leaves sometimes speckled gray or silver.
Zones: 3-9: see indiviual species
Spacing: 10-12″ (25-30cm)
Propagation: seed, division

P. angustifolia (an-goos-ti-FOH-li-a)
Blue Lungwort
Loose clusters of blue tubular flowers open from pink buds. Height 9-12″ (23-30cm). Foliage green. Zones 2-8.

P. saccharata (sa-ka-RAH-ta)
Bethlehem Sage
Buds pink, mature flowers blue. Height 9-18″ (23-45cm). Gray-speckled leaves persist long into fall, are sometimes evergreen. Cultivars:
   'Margery Fish': more vigorous than species.
   'Mrs. Moon': big, silver-spotted leaves.
   'Sissinghurst White': flowers white; silvery marking on leaves.

PULSATILLA (pul-sa-TIL-a) ◑
Pulsatilla vulgaris (vul-GAH-ris)
[*Anemone pulsatilla* (a-NEM-oh-nee)]
European Pasqueflower
Spring flowering perennial for edging or rock garden. Big 2″ (5cm), bell-shaped blue or reddish-purple flowers top 8-12″ (20-30cm) stems. Characteristic fuzzy fruits persist after flowering. Foliage develops after flowers; finely divided, fern-like leaves mound 8-10″ (20-25cm).
Zones: 5-7
Spacing: 10-12″ (25-30cm)
Propagation: (root cuttings) leave undisturbed if possible

○ = Full Sun		♠ = Evergreen	
◑ = Partial Shade		**N** = Native or Naturalized Plant	
● = Shade		⚐ = Ornamental Grass	
⌇ = Groundcover		✂ = Cut Flowers	

Rodgersia aesculifolia

Rosmarinus officinalis

RANUNCULUS (ra-NUN-kew-lus) ◑●⤳ N
Buttercup, Crowfoot
R. repens (REE-pens)
Butter Daisy, Creeping Buttercup
Vigorous spreader has bright yellow summer flowers. Prefers moist soil. Use for informal groundcover. Naturalized species, may become invasive. Leaves mound 6-12″ (15-30cm). Flowering stems 18-24″ (45-60cm) tall.
Cultivar **'Pleniflorus'** (plee-ni-FLOH-rus) ['Flore Pleno' (FLOH-re PLEE-noh)]: less vigorous than species, growing to 18″ (45cm), with double yellow flowers.
Zones: 3-8
Spacing: 15-18″ (38-45cm)
Propagation: division, seed

> Remove winter mulch carefully to avoid damaging tender young shoots. If a late frost threatens, cover plants with newspapers or another temporary protective cover. And apply early fertilizer to the soil not the leaves whose delicate tissues will be burned.

RODGERSIA (rod-JER-si-a) ○◑
R. aesculifolia (es-kew-li-FOH-li-a)
Fingerleaf Rodgersia
Rhizomatous perennial with bold compound leaves. Late spring spires of white or pinkish blossoms. Height 3-6′ (0.9-1.8m). Prefers moist, boggy soil. Leaves often bronze-green, stems clothed with brown hairs. Flower clusters 18-24″ (45-60cm) long. Tolerates full sun only where soil can remain constantly moist.
Zones: 5-6
Spacing: 18-24″ (45-60cm)
Propagation: division in spring

ROSMARINUS (rohz-ma-REE-nus) ○◑♠
R. officinalis (o-fi-si-NAH-lis)
Rosemary
Tender, shrubby evergreen herb. Height 24-36″ (60-90cm). Best in well-drained, slightly acid or neutral soil. Gray-green, aromatic, needle-like leaves have many culinary uses. Late winter or early spring flowers are violet-blue, sometimes white. Trim in spring and after flowering to encourage fresh leafy growth.
Zones: 7-10
Spacing: 24-36″ (60-90cm)
Propagation: cuttings

Rudbeckia hirta

Ruta graveolens

Sagina subulata

RUDBECKIA (rud-BEK-i-a) ◐ ◑ ✕ N
Coneflower
Tall, showy, long-lasting blossoms from mid-summer to fall. Rapid growth in fertile, loose soil. Easy to grow in borders, natural plantings. Daisy flowers have yellow to orange petals and dark, high central cones.
Zones: 3-10
Spacing: 12-15″ (30-38cm)
Propagation: seed, division in spring

R. fulgida (FUL-ji-da)
Black-eyed Susan, Orange or Showy Coneflower
Summer flowering plant grows to 18-30″ (45-75cm).
Cultivars:
 'Goldstrum': compact and free-flowering; grows to 24″ (60cm), big dark yellow flowers. Does not come true from seed.
 'Goldquelle': lemon-yellow double flowers.

R. hirta (HER-ta)
Black-eyed Susan
Short-lived perennial often grown as annual or biennial. Height to 36″ (90cm). Deep yellow 2-3″ (5-8cm) flowers.

RUTA (ROO-ta) ◐ ◑ ♠
R. graveolens (gra-VEE-oh-lens)
Rue, Herb-of-grace
Shrubby herb grows to 12-36″ (30-90cm). Lacy, aromatic, blue-green foliage. Best in moist, light, well-drained soil. Useful foliage plant in border, herb garden, or as low hedge in milder climates. Summer flower clusters pale yellow. Trim back to old wood in spring to encourage fresh bushy growth.
Note: leaves may cause dermatitis.
Zones: 4-9
Spacing: 12-18″ (30-45cm)
Propagation: seed, cuttings, division

SAGINA (sa-GEE-na) ◐ ◑ ● ⋙ ♠
S. subulata (soo-bew-LAH-ta)
Corsican Pearlwort
Moss-like evergreen perennial. Suitable for shady locations. Small white flowers are produced on short stalks in mid-summer. Small leaves form dense mats of foliage. Grows 2-4″ (5-10cm).
Zones: 4-10
Spacing: 8-10″ (20-25cm)
Propagation: division

Salvia azurea

Salvia officinalis 'Tricolor'

Salvia officinalis

Salvia × *superba* 'May Night'

SALVIA (SAL-vi-a) ○
Sage, Ramona

Reliable border plants with blue- or gray-green leaves and summer or fall flowers from lavender to purple. Best in average to dry, acid, well-drained soil. Useful in borders, natural plantings, smaller varieties for rock gardens. Foliage and flowers often aromatic.

Zones: see individual species
Spacing: 15-18″ (38-45cm)
Propagation: seed, division, cuttings

S. azurea (a-ZEW-ree-a) **N**
Blue Sage, Azure Sage

Fall-flowering, grows to 3-4′ (0.9-1.2m). Dark green leaves larger at stem base. Azure-blue flowers borne in axils of smaller upper leaves, forming loose spikes. Zones 5-9.
S. a. var. grandiflora [*S. pitcheri* (PICH-er-y)] has paler green bigger leaves, lighter colored flowers.

S. officinalis (o-fi-si-NAH-lis)
Common Sage, Garden Sage

Shrubby, semi-evergreen culinary herb has fuzzy 2″ (5cm) gray-green leaves. Mounds 18-24″ (45-60cm). Some forms have variegated foliage. Flowers small; purple, blue, or white. Zones 4-9.

S. pratensis (pra-TEN-sis)
[*S. haematodes* (hee-ma-TOH-deez)]
Meadow Clary, Meadow Sage

Bright lavender-blue flower spikes top 12-36″ (30-90cm) plants in summer. Long-stemmed basal leaves; few small leaves on flowering stems. Remove spent flowers to promote second blooming. Tuberous species grows best in evenly moist soil. Zones 3-9.

S. × *superba* (soo-PER-ba)
[*S. nemorosa* (ne-mo-ROH-sa)]
Violet Sage, Hybrid Sage

Dense spikes of violet or violet-blue summer flowers rise 18″ (45cm) to 4′ (1.2m). Taller varieties need support. Zones 4-7.
Cultivars:
  'Blue Queen': rich violet flowers, height 18-24″ (45-60cm); tolerates heat and drought.
  'East Friesland': deep purple flowers, compact plants grow without support to 18″ (45cm).
  'May Night': larger, deep indigo blue flowers; height to 18″ (45cm).

Sanguinaria canadensis

Santolina chamaecyparissus

Sanguisorba canadensis

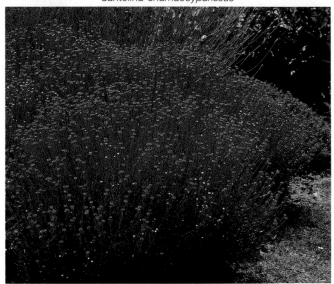
Santolina virens

SANGUINARIA (san-gwi-NAH-ri-a) ○ ◑ **N**
S. canadensis (ka-na-DEN-sis)
Bloodroot
Woodland plant with white early spring blossoms and scalloped, roundish leaves. Grows 6-12″ (15-30cm). Best in moist yet well-drained, acid, humus-rich soil in partial shade. Use in woodland, natural planting. Sap, stems, and rhizomes red.
Note: sap contains bitter alkaloid that affects muscles and nerves if swallowed or absorbed.
Zones: 3-9
Spacing: 10-15″ (25-38cm)
Propagation: seed, division

SANGUISORBA (san-gwi-SOR-ba) ○ ◑ **N**
Burnet
S. canadensis (ka-na-DEN-sis)
Canadian Burnet, Great Burnet, American Burnet
Large clump-forming perennial for moist locations. Summer to fall, white bottlebrush-like flowers rise 4-5′ (1.2-1.5m). Grows vigorously in cool, damp soil. Useful in damp border, beside stream or pond, in boggy natural area. Leaves compound, many sharply toothed leaflets.
Zones: 3-8
Spacing: 18-13″ (45-60cm)
Propagation: seed, division

SANTOLINA (san-toh-LEE-na) ○ ↝ ▲
Compact, shrubby plants with aromatic finely-divided foliage. Grow best in well-drained soil; tolerate heat. Useful edging, low hedge, groundcover, or rock garden plants. Small, yellow, button-like flower heads in summer. Trim after flowering to maintain shape; prune older plants hard in spring.
Zones: 6-8
Spacing: 18-24″ (45-60cm)
Propagation: cuttings (summer)

S. chamaecyparissus (ka-mee-si-pa-RIS-us)
[*S. incana* (in-KAH-na)]
Lavender Cotton
Gray-green foliage mounds 12-24″ (30-60cm). Useful groundcover plant for poor, stony soils. Prefers dry heat. Prune after flowering to shape new growth.

S. virens (VY-rens)
[also called *S. rosmarinifolia* (rohz-ma-ree-ni-FOH-li-a)]
Green Lavender Cotton, Holy Flax
Spreading sub-shrub has dark green, smooth foliage. Height to 24″. Makes good low hedge.

Saponaria ocymoides

Satureja montana

Scabiosa caucasica

SAPONARIA (sa-poh-NAH-ri-a) ○ ➤➤
Soapwort
S. ocymoides (oh-ki-MOI-deez)
Rock Soapwort
Trailing, mat-forming groundcover for dry, stony places. Height 4-9″ (10-23cm). Good for banks, edgings, walls, or rock gardens. Flat, semi-evergreen leaves. Showy, bright pink clusters of summer blossoms. Trim back hard after flowering to encourage compact new growth.
Zones: 2-7
Spacing: 9-12″ (23-30cm)
Propagation: seed, division, cuttings

SATUREJA (sa-tew-REE-ya) ○
Savory, Calamint
S. montana (mon-TAH-na)
Winter Savory
Low-growing aromatic herb does well in any well-drained soil. Height 6-12″ (15-30cm). Smooth, shiny leaves. Tender young leaves and stem tips used to flavor foods. Summer flowers are white, pink, or purplish. Mint family.
Zones: 5-10
Spacing: 4-6″ (10-15cm)
Propagation: seed, division, cuttings

SCABIOSA (skay-bee-OH-sa) ○ ✄
S. caucasica (kaw-KAS-i-ka)
Caucasian Scabious, Scabious, Pincushion Flower
Late summer flowers like small pincushions, in white and shades of blue. Best in moist, well-drained, neutral to alkaline soil, in humid climate. Plant groups in border for best display. Lower leaves provide dense gray-green foil for flowers that rise to 18-30″ (45-75cm). Excellent cut flower.
Zones: 3-7
Spacing: 12-15″ (30-38cm)
Propagation: seed, division

New herbaceous perennials are planted once the soil becomes workable in early spring. Many established ones can also be lifted and divided now. The outer edges of old clumps whose displays are weakened through overcrowding will become established faster and give better results than the woody centers of the same clumps.

Sedum acre

Sedum spectabile 'Autumn Joy'

Sedum kamtschaticum

Sedum spurium 'Dragon's Blood'

SEDUM (SEE-dum) ○ ⋙ ♠
Stonecrop, Orpine

Easy succulents with fleshy leaves and clusters of blossoms that attract butterflies. Prefer fertile, well-drained soil. Tolerant of infertile conditions. Many species also tolerate drought and heat. Fine for rock garden, edging, some in borders.

Zones: 3-10
Spacing: 18-24″ (45-60cm)
Propagation: seed, division, cuttings (stem and leaf)

S. acre (AH-kree)
Golden-carpet, Goldmoss Stonecrop

Spreads vigorously with trailing stems. Mounds 2-3″ (5-8cm) high. Useful filler between stepping or paving stones. Tiny pale green scale-like leaves cover stems. Spring flowers golden-yellow.

S. album (AL-bum)
Wormgrass, White Stonecrop

Creeping spreader mounds 3-8″ (8-20cm). Early summer white flowers in flat-topped panicles.

S. kamtschaticum (kamt-SHAT-i-kum)
Kamschatca Stonecrop, Orange Stonecrop

Spreading, unbranched pale green stems bear 1½″ (4cm) darker leaves that turn bronze in fall. Mounds 4-9″ (10-23cm). Useful in dry wall. Summer flowers yellow to orange, in sparse flat clusters.

S. k. subsp. ellacombianum (e-la-kom-bee-AH-num) has scalloped leaf margins and bright yellow or lemon-yellow flowers on 4-6″ (10-15cm) mounds.

S. k. subsp. middendorffianum (mid-en-dorf-ee-AH-num) has dark green, needle-like leaves and bright yellow flowers on 4-6″ (10-15cm) mounds.

S. oreganum (o-ree-GAH-num) N
Oregon Stonecrop

Clump-forming succulent with red-tinted foliage that turns completely red in hot climate. Height to 6″ (15cm). Late spring yellow flowers fade to pale pink.

S. sieboldii (see-BOHL-dee-y)
October Daphne, October Plant

Spreading plant mounds 6-9″ (15-23cm). Rounded 1″ (2.5cm) leaves in groups of three on trailing stems. Late summer pink flowers. Early frost may prevent flowering. Good at front of borders.

Sempervivum

SEDUM (cont'd)

S. spectabile (spek-TAH-bi-lee)
Showy Stonecrop, Showy Sedum
Clusters of showy red or pink flowers top attractive gray-green foliage in late summer. Height 18-24″ (45-60cm). Tolerates partial shade. Grows in dry soil. Useful sedum for borders, edging.
Cultivars:
  'Autumn Joy': grows to 24″ (60cm) with densely clustered pink to rusty-red flowers; tolerates moist soils.
  'Brilliant': raspberry-red flowers on 18″ (45cm) plants.

S. spurium (SPEW-ri-um)
Two-row Stonecrop
Vigorous spreader forms dense mats mounding 2-6″ (5-15cm). Trailing reddish stems root readily, develop new ascending stem clusters. Grows in dry soil. Red-edged younger foliage turns deeper red in fall. White to rose summer flower clusters rise 4″ (10cm) or more over leafy clumps. Good sedum for borders, edging; excellent groundcover.
Cultivars:
  'Bronze Carpet': bronze foliage mounds to 4″ (10cm); pink flowers.
  'Dragon's Blood': purplish foliage; grows 3-4″ (8-10cm) high; flowers dark red.
  'Red Carpet': brilliant red foliage mounds 3-4″ (8-10cm); red flowers.

S. × 'Vera Jameson'
Hybrid sedum with waxy, bluish to mahogany-red foliage and 4″ (10cm) clusters of dusky pink flowers. Height 10-12″ (25-30cm).

SEMPERVIVUM (sem-per-VEE-vum) ○ ᴍᴡ ♠
Houseleek, Live-forever, Hen-and-chickens
Easy, adaptable stoloniferous succulents with symmetrical leafy rosettes and loose spikes of white, green, yellow, rosy, or purple summer blossoms. Best in well-drained sandy or gritty soil. Useful in containers, rock or wall gardens, on stony banks, as groundcover. Rosettes die after flowering but are replaced by offsets. Many species and cultivars have green, red-marked, or entirely red foliage.
S. arachnoideum (a-rak-NOI-dee-um), **Spiderweb** or **Cobweb Houseleek,** has dense webbing of gray threads over pale green leafy rosettes.
Zones: 5-9
Spacing: 8-10 (20-25cm)
Propagation: division, seed

Sidalcea

× Solidaster luteus

Solidago

Stachys byzantina

SIDALCEA (si-DAL-see-a) ○ ✕ **N**
Checker-mallow, Prairie Mallow
Summer-flowering perennial with hollyhock-like blossoms. Height ranges from 18″ (45cm) to 4′ (1.2m). Grows best in well-drained soil. Useful in borders, natural plantings. Foliage lobed, divided. White, rose, or pink flowers on branching spikes. Named garden varieties developed from native species.
Zones: 5-9
Spacing: 15-18″ (38-45cm)
Propagation: seed (species), division (hybrids, cultivars)

SOLIDAGO (so-li-DAH-goh) ○ ✕ **N**
Goldenrod
Vigorous summer- to fall-flowering perennial for informal borders and natural plantings. Cultivar heights 1-5′ (0.3-1.5m). Good in moist, well-drained soil. Clusters of tiny yellow or white blossoms. Species readily self-seeding, may become invasive. Tolerates dry soil.
Zones: 3-10
Spacing: 18″ (45cm)
Propagation: seed, division

✕ *SOLIDASTER* (so-li-DAS-stur) ○ ✕
✕ *S. luteus* (LOO-tee-us)
[✕ *S. hybridus* (HYB-ri-dus)]
Hybrid Goldenrod
Intergeneric hybrid from *Solidago* and *Aster* produces clusters of small yellow daisies from mid-summer. Height to 30″ (75cm). Best in well-drained soil. Good in borders, natural plantings.
Zones: 5-9
Spacing: 18-24″ (45-60cm)
Propagation: division

STACHYS (STAK-is) ○ ⋙ ♠
Betony, Hedge Nettle, Woundwort
S. byzantina (bi-zan-TEE-na)
[*S. lanata* (la-NAH-ta)]
Woolly Betony, Lamb's-ears
Velvety spreading foliage forms mat 12-15″ (30-38cm) high. Best in moist yet well-drained soil. Good edging, rock garden, groundcover plant. Big, white-woolly leaves resemble lamb's ears. Spikes of pink to purple flowers in spring. Tolerates shade in dry soil.
Zones: 4-8
Spacing: 12-18″ (30-45cm)
Propagation: seed, division

Stokesia laevis

Symphytum caucasicum

Tanacetum vulgare

STOKESIA (STOHK-si-a) ○ ◑ ✕ ⋙ N
S. laevis (LEE-vis)
Stokes' Aster
Easily grown border plant provides year-round dark green foliage and 1-4″ (2.5-10cm) blooms in summer. Height 12-24″ (30-60cm). Best in sandy, well-drained soil. Plant in groups for best display. Flowers blue to purple, with named cultivars in white and shades of blue.
Zones: 5-9
Spacing: 12-15″ (30-38cm)
Propagation: seed, division in spring

SYMPHYTUM (SIM-fi-tum) ◑
Comfrey
Vigorous clump-forming perennials suitable for natural planting or informal border. Best in moist soils. Large basal leaves, smaller upper ones. Flowers borne in loose branching clusters.
Zones: 4-8
Spacing: 12-18″ (30-45cm)
Propagation: division, seed

S. caucasicum (kaw-KAS-i-kum)
Blue Comfrey
Upright plants with soft hairy foliage and spring flowers opening pink, then turning blue. Remove spent blooms to extend flowering. Height 18-36″ (45-90cm).

S. grandiflorum (gran-di-FLOH-rum) ⋙
Large-flowered Comfrey, Groundcover Comfrey
Rapidly spreading rhizomatous plant with shiny leaves and stems that rise 10-15″ (25-38cm). Spring flowers creamy-yellow. Tolerates dry conditions.

TANACETUM (ta-na-SEE-tum) ○ ◑ N
Tansy
T. vulgare (vul-GAH-ree)
Common Tansy, Golden-buttons
Naturalized herb grown for its yellow button flowers and deeply cut, ferny, aromatic foliage. Height to 36″ (90cm). Grows in any well-drained soil. Useful as border filler, in herb garden, natural planting. Flowers in summer.
Note: leaves and stems are poisonous except in extremely small quantities.
Zones: 3-9
Spacing: 18-24″ (45-60cm)
Propagation: seed, division

Teucrium chamaedrys

Thymus ✕ *citriodorus*

Thalictrum dipterocarpum

TEUCRIUM   (TEW-kri-um)   ○ ⋙ ♠
Germander

T. chamaedrys   (ka-MEE-dris)
Wall Germander
Compact, shrubby, aromatic evergreen with shiny oval leaves. Height
10-15″ (25-38cm). Best in moist yet well-drained soil. Useful as low
hedge, at front of border, for edging. Shear or trim for formal shape.
Late summer flowers rose-purple. Tolerates some shade.
Cultivar **'Prostratum'** (pros-TRAH-tum) is a good groundcover plant,
grows 6-10″ (15-25cm). Rose-pink flowers.
Zones: 5-9
Spacing: 6-12″ (15-30cm)
Propagation: seed, division

THALICTRUM   (tha-LIK-tum)   ○ ◑ ✄
Meadow Rue
Elegant plants with airy divided foliage and fluffy blossoms in late
spring and summer. Best in moist, rich soil. Useful light contrast in
borders, for edge of woodland, close to water.
Zones: 5-8
Spacing: 15-18″ (38-45cm)
Propagation: seed, division

T. aquilegifolium   (ak-wi-lee-ji-FOH-li-um)
Columbine Meadow Rue
Clump-forming with masses of bluish columbine-like leaves. Height
24-36″ (60-90cm). Late spring lilac-blue flowers in 6-8″ (15-20cm)
clusters. Cultivars have white, orangish, or blue-purple blossoms. Male
and female flowers on separate plants. Tolerates heat.

T. delavayi   (de-la-VAY-y)
Yunnan Meadow Rue
Graceful, slender stems rise 2-4′ (0.6-1.2m). Fern-like foliage. Airy,
lilac-and-cream flower clusters in summer. Provide support for flowering stems.

T. dioicum   (dy-OH-i-kum)   **N**
Early Meadow Rue
Dainty native for natural plantings in moist locations. Height 12-24″
(30-60cm). Early summer blossoms creamy-white, in 12″ (30cm) fluffy
clusters. Male and female flowers on separate plants.

T. dipterocarpum   (dip-te-roh-KAR-pum)
Yunnan Meadow Rue
Airy sprays of mauve to lilac flowers with yellow stamens are produced
late summer. Lovely fern-like foliage.

Thermopsis caroliniana

Thymus serpyllum

THERMOPSIS (thur-MOP-sis) ✂ N
False Lupine
T. caroliniana (ka-ro-li-nee-AH-na)
Carolina Lupine
Long-lived, sprawling perennial has yellow spring flowers on compact, upright spikes resembling lupines. Height 2½-4′ (0.75-1.2m). Good in border, natural planting. Leaves blue-green, divided. Tolerates some shade. Resists drought.
Zones: 3-9
Spacing: 24-36″ (60-90cm)
Propagation: division in spring, seed (sow as soon as ripe in late summer)

THYMUS (TY-mus) ○◑ ᙡ ♣
Thyme
Low-growing aromatic herbs with shrubby, sprawling to upright stems. Best in light, well-drained, acid soil. Useful in rock garden, herb garden, as edging, and as groundcover on banks and in no-traffic areas. Small, shiny oval leaves. Rose or lilac flowers in early summer.
Zones: 4-10
Spacing: 10-12″ (25-30cm)
Propagation: seed, division

T. × citriodorus (sit-ree-o-DOH-rus)
Lemon Thyme
Many-branched, semi-trailing plant grows 4-12″ (10-30cm) high. Lemon scented. Tiny leaves, pale purple flowers. Cut back in spring to encourage fresh compact growth.

T. pseudolanuginosus (soo-doh-la-new-gi-NOH-sus)
Woolly Thyme
Sprawling shrubby evergreen forms undulating mat 2-3″ (5-8cm) high. Gray woolly foliage covers stems. Pinkish flowers rare.

T. serpyllum (ser-PIL-lum)
Mother-of-thyme, Wild Thyme
Rooting, spreading stems with small upright branches form mat 2-6″ (5-15cm) high. Roundish, dark green leaves, used for seasoning and in pot-pourri. Small purplish-white flower clusters in summer.

Tiarella wherryi

Tricyrtis hirta

Tradescantia virginiana

TIARELLA (tee-a-REL-a) ◐ ● ⌇ ♠ N
False Miterwort
Low maintenance groundcover for shade and rich, moist soils. Broad leaves provide foil for profuse clusters of spring or summer flowers.
Zones: 4-8
Spacing: 12-15″ (30-38cm)
Propagation: division, seed

T. cordifolia (kor-di-FOH-li-a)
Foamflower, Allegheny Foamflower
Lobed, heart-shaped leaves have burgundy coloring along veins in spring and fall, may turn entirely bronze in winter. Rapidly spreading stoloniferous plants mound 6-12″ (15-30cm) high. Delicate pink flower buds open to long-lasting creamy-white spring flowers.

T. wherryi (WE-ree-y)
Foamflower
Lobed leaves turn reddish in winter. Slow to spread, clump-forming plants mound 4-10″ (10-25cm). Summer flowers in white, airy clusters.

TRADESCANTIA (tra-des-KAN-shi-a) ○ ◐ N
T. virginiana (vir-ji-nee-AH-na)
Spiderwort, Widow's Tears
Reliable, grass-like perennial for borders, natural plantings, partly shaded woodland locations. Stems sprawl and rise to 12-24″ (30-60cm). Prefers fertile, well-drained soil. Tolerates dry conditions. Short-lived flowers in white and shades of blue to purple open from late spring to mid-summer.
Zones: 4-9
Spacing: 12-15″ (30-38cm)
Propagation: division in spring, seed

TRICYRTIS (try-KUR-tis) ◐ ●
Toad Lily
T. hirta (HIR-ta)
Toad Lily, Hairy Toad Lily, Japanese Toad Lily
Late summer or fall flowering rhizomatous lily grows 24-36″ (60-90cm) high. Best in rich, moist yet well-drained soil. Grows well in container, border, rock garden. Arching stems clothed with clasping, soft-hairy foliage. Flowers white to lilac with darker spots and blotches.
Zones: 4-8
Spacing: 18-24″ (45-60cm)
Propagation: division in spring, seed

Trillium grandiflorum

Trollius ledebourii

Verbena rigida

TRILLIUM (TRIL-i-um) ◑ ● N
T. grandiflorum (gran-di-FLOH-rum)
Snow Trillium, Wake-robin, Great White Trillium
Showy three-petaled spring flowers top leafy 9-18″ (23-45cm) stems. Must have rich, moist soil and at least partial shade. Plant in woodland, shaded border, or natural area. Flower opens white, fades to pink and rose. Clump-forming. Plant rhizomes about 4″ (10cm) deep.
Zones: 4-9
Spacing: 12″ (30cm)
Propagation: division, seed (slow to germinate)

TROLLIUS (TROL-i-us) ○ ◑ ✄
Globeflower
T. ledebourii (le-de-BOOR-ee-y)
Ledebour Globeflower
Large orange buttercup flowers in spring on 24-36″ (60-90cm) stems. Best in moist, heavy soil and cool climate. Useful in boggy meadow, natural planting, shaded border, at edge of pond or stream. Deep-cut leaves mound under flowering stems. Vigorous.
Zones: 3-6
Spacing: 10-12″ (25-30cm)
Propagation: seed, division

VERBENA (ver-BEE-na) ○ ⋙ ♠ N
V. rigida (RIG-i-da)
[**V. venosa** (ve-NOH-sa)]
Vervain
Free-flowering tender perennial is both heat and drought tolerant. Spreads with creeping, rooting stems. Upright growth to 12-24″ (30-60cm). Best in well-drained soils. Useful as edging, in rock garden. Clusters of blue to purple flowers from summer to fall. Naturalized.
Zones: 8-10
Spacing: 18-24″ (45-60cm)
Propagation: cuttings, seed

○ = Full Sun	♠ = Evergreen
◑ = Partial Shade	N = Native or Naturalized Plant
● = Shade	✠ = Ornamental Grass
⋙ = Groundcover	✄ = Cut Flowers

Veronica latifolia 'Crater Lake Blue'

Veronica repens 'Alba'

Veronica spicata

VERONICA (ve-RON-i-ka) ○◑
Speedwell, Brooklime
Clump-forming or spreading perennials with blue, white, or rose flowers in clusters or spikes. Best in well-drained soil. Useful plants for border, edging, rock garden, groundcover, or for cutting. Remove faded blossoms to encourage more flower development.
Zones: see individual species
Spacing: 12-18″ (30-45cm)
Propagation: division, seed, cuttings

V. incana (in-KAH-na) ✂
Woolly Speedwell
Silvery-gray woolly foliage and stems, blue summer flowers. Height 12-18″ (30-45cm). Intolerant of extreme heat or high humidity. Zones 3-7.

V. latifolia (la-ti-FOH-li-a) 〰
[*V. teucrium* (TEW-kri-um)]
Hungarian Speedwell
Spreading groundcover grows 6-20″ (15-50cm) high. Blue spring flowers. Zones 3-7.
Cultivar **'Crater Lake Blue'** is compact form with bright blue flowers; height 12-15″ (30-38cm).

V. longifolia (lon-ji-FOH-lia) ✂ **N**
[*V. maritima* (ma-RIT-i-ma)]
Long-leaf Veronica
Clump-forming, naturalized species has smooth stems, grows to 2-4′ (0.6-1.2m). Useful in border and for cutting. Lilac summer flowers in 12″ (30cm) spikes. Zones 4-8.

V. prostrata (pros-TRAH-ta) 〰
[*V. rupestris* (roo-PES-tris)]
Harebell Speedwell
Dense, mat-forming plant with flowering stems rising to 8″ (20cm) over gray-green foliage. Blue spring flower clusters. Zones 5-8.

V. repens (REE-pens) 〰
Creeping Speedwell
Prostrate stems form mound 4″ (10cm) high. Moss-like, lustrous foliage. Rose to bluish spring flowers in small groups. Zones. 5-8.

V. spicata (spee-KAH-ta) ✂
Spike Speedwell
Clump-forming, grows to 10-36″ (25-90cm). Glossy foliage. Blue flowers in dense 12-36″ (30-90cm) spikes. Varieties have flowers in white, shades of blue, rarely pink. Zones 3-8.

Vinca minor

Viola cornuta

VINCA (VIN-ka) ○ ◑ ● ⌇ ♠

Periwinkle

Spreading, trailing woody vines bear glossy dark green leaves. Grow in any well-drained soil, dies back in drought. Useful container plants, groundcover for shaded areas such as banks, edging. Flowers freely in sun, from early spring.

Zones: see individual species

Spacing: 12″ (30cm)

Propagation: division, layers, cuttings, seed

V. major (MAY-jor)

Greater Periwinkle, Blue-buttons, Band Plant

Tender creeper for seasonal containers in the north. Mounds 12-18″ (30-45cm). Large 2-3″ (5-8cm) leaves. Bright blue flowers. Zones 7-9.

V. minor (MY-nor) **N**

Common Periwinkle, Myrtle

Prostrate stems root as they spread, bear 1½″ (4cm) elliptical leaves. Vigorous, tolerant, naturalized perennial has cultivars with white or blue to purple flowers, variegated foliage. Zones 4-10.

VIOLA (VY-oh-la) ○ ◑ ✂

Violet

Low-growing, tufted or clump-forming perennials. Distinctive fragrant flowers in spring. Prefer moist, well-drained soil. Useful as edging, on banks, in rock garden, natural planting, moist woodland sites.

Zones: 4-9: see individual species

Spacing: 6-8″ (15-20cm)

Propagation: division, seed

V. canadensis (ka-na-DEN-sis) **N**

Canada Violet

Fragrant purple-tinged white flowers with yellow eye. Height to 12″ (30cm). Best in shaded locations. Hardy to Zone 3.

V. cornuta (kor-NEW-ta)

Horned Violet, Viola, Tufted Pansy

Spring flowers violet-blue; cultivars have larger flowers in white, yellow, apricot, red, and purple shades. Main stems tend to sprawl, then rise to 4-12″ (10-30cm). Cut back after flowering to encourage second bloom in fall. Vigorous tender perennial often grown as annual bedding plant. Evergreen and hardy to zone 6.

Viola cucullata 'Freckles'

Viola odorata

Waldsteinia ternata

VIOLA (cont'd)

V. cucullata (koo-kew-LAH-ta) **N**
[*V. obliqua* (oh-BLEE-ka)]
Marsh Blue Violet
Violet flowers rise 3-6″ (8-15cm). Pale, undulating leaves 3-4″ (8-10cm) wide. Tufted growth from scaly rhizomes. Hardy to zone 5.

V. odorata (oh-do-RAH-ta) ⋙
Sweet Violet
Fragrant spring flower blooms violet, rose, or white. Height 2-8″ (5-20cm). Broad oval or kidney-shaped leaves. Spreads rapidly with long runners. Self-seeding; semi-evergreen. Hardy to zone 6.

V. pedata (pe-DAH-ta) **N**
Bird-foot Violet
Clump-forming, grows to 2-6″ (5-15cm). Needs well-drained, sandy soil and shade. Leaves palmately divided, like birds'-feet. Dark purple upper petals, pale lilac lower ones; cultivars have white, violet blossoms.

V. pubescens (pew-BES-enz) **N**
Downy Yellow Violet
Softly hairy stems and foliage, with most leaves near stem tips. Height 8-12″ (20-30cm). Bright yellow flowers in spring. Best in rich dry soil, shade, and cooler climate of zones 3-7.

WALDSTEINIA (vald-STY-ni-a) ○◐●⋙▲
Easy, spreading strawberry-like groundcovers with dry, inedible fruits. Yellow flowers in late spring, early summer. Best in well-drained soil. Useful in rock gardens, as groundcover. Creeping rhizomes, semi-evergreen foliage.
Zones: 4-7
Spacing: 8-12″ (20-30cm)
Propagation: division

W. fragarioides (fra-gah-ree-OI-deez) **N**
Barren Strawberry
Forms spreading mat 4-6″ (10-15cm) high.

W. ternata (ter-NAH-ta)
[*W. trifolia* (try-FOH-li-a)]
Siberian Barren Strawberry
Compact and spreading. Leafy rosettes rise to 4″ (10cm). Useful on banks.

If woody shrubs and trees need added water during open, dry winters, water exposed herbaceous perennials as well.

Yucca filamentosa

YUCCA (YOO-ka) ○ ♠ N

Stemless or short-stemmed shrubs provide year-round value as accent in border or as single or grouped specimens. Best in well-drained sandy loam. Dramatic, sword-like succulent leaves in basal rosette from which rise showy clusters of fragrant white or creamy blossoms in summer.

Zones: 4-10
Spacing: 24-36″ (60-90cm)
Propagation: seed, offsets

Y. filamentosa (fi-la-men-TOH-sa)
Adam's-needle
Leafy rosette grows to 36″ (90cm). Arching flower stems usually rise 4-5′ (1.2-1.5m), sometimes as high as 15′ (4.5m). Creamy-white, pendulous blossoms.

Y. glauca (GLAW-ka)
Soapweed
Short, prostrate stems give rise to clumps of pale green foliage rising to 36″ (90cm). Leaves have white or brown margins. Green-white flowers in 30″ (75cm) clusters.

INDEX

INDEX (cont'd)

INDEX (cont'd)

INDEX

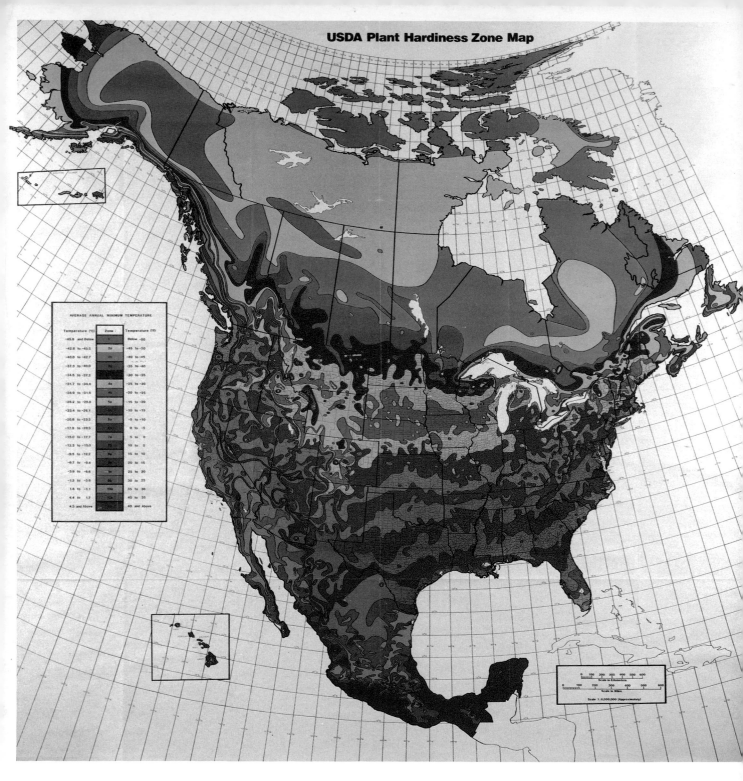

USDA Plant Hardiness Zone Map

The USDA Plant Hardiness Zone Map shows in detail the lowest temperatures that can be expected each year in the United States, Canada and Mexico. The map shows 11 different zones, each of which represents an area of winter hardiness for the plants of agriculture and our natural landscape. Zones 2-10 in the map have been subdivided into light- and dark-colored sections (a and b) that represent 5°F (2.8°C) differences within the 10°F (5.6°C) zone. The light color of each zone represents the colder section; the darker color, the warmer section. Zone 11 represents any area where the average annual minimum temperature is above 40°F (4.4°C). The map shows 2° latitude and longitude lines. Areas above an arbitrary elevation are traditionally considered unsuitable for planting and do not bear zone designations. There are also island zones that, because of elevation differences, are warmer or cooler than the surrounding areas and are given a different zone designation. Many large urban areas carry a warmer zone designation than the surrounding countryside. This map should only be used as a general guide. Plants may vary in their growth habits from area to area within the same zone.